Annabel Karmel's SUPERFOODS for Babies and Children

Annabel Karmel's
SUPERFOODS
for Babies and Children

From the best-selling author of THE NEW COMPLETE BABY AND TODDLER MEAL PLANNER

With Consultant Nutritionist Paul Sacher, Specialist Clinical Dietitian,
GREAT ORMOND STREET CHILDREN'S HOSPITAL

EBURY PRESS
LONDON

First published in 2001

5 7 9 10 8 6

Text copyright © Annabel Karmel 2001
Photographs copyright © Daniel Pangbourne 2001, except p. 55
Dave King 2004

First published by Ebury Press
Random House, 20 Vauxhall Bridge Road, London SW1V 2SA

Random House Australia (Pty) Limited
20 Alfred Street, Milsons Point, Sydney, New South Wales 2061, Australia

Random House New Zealand Limited
18 Poland Road, Glenfield, Auckland 10, New Zealand

Random House South Africa (Pty) Limited
Endulini, 5A Jubilee Road, Parktown 2193, South Africa

The Random House Group Limited Reg. No. 954009

www.randomhouse.co.uk

A CIP catalogue record for this book is available from the British Library

ISBN 9780091879020

Editor: Emma Callery
Designer: Helen Lewis
Photographer: Daniel Pangbourne, except p. 55 by Dave King
Stylist: Tessa Evelegh
Home economist: Sarah Lewis
Illustrator: Nadine Wickenden

Originated in Italy by Colorlito
Printed and bound in Singapore

contents

introduction

Feeding children can be one of the most frustrating aspects of child rearing. As parents we all start off with the best of intentions, but all too soon we find that our two-year-old only wants Thomas The Tank Engine spaghetti or dinosaur chicken nuggets, and our six-year-old only eats Cocoa Pops. Frazzled to the core we are all tempted to give in to the seductive television/magazine advertising where the perfect baby/child is seen remorselessly gobbling the last mouthful of a proprietary brand. It's shocking that at a time when diet is most crucial to health, the label 'children's food' represents some of the worst quality, most unhealthy food on offer.

Many children go through a stage when all they seem to do is eat just a few foods or simply pick at their meal and push away the plate. The problem often seems to be that the more we coax our children into eating, the more stubborn they become and the less they eat. Toddler power comes of age!

It is now clear that a junk food diet, which is high in fat, sugar and salt, can lead to health problems like obesity, diabetes, heart disease and cancer later in life. So many of us will die from diet-related diseases, but by setting up a good diet in the vital first few years you will help protect your child's future. Studies are now beginning to show that chronic diseases like heart disease take root early in life. Having lost my first child Natasha due to a rare viral infection when she was very young, I was determined that my three children would grow up to enjoy eating good healthy food since what they stuffed into their mouths was within my orbit of control and I felt I could make a difference.

Following Natasha's death, I wanted to channel my grief into something positive but it wasn't until a year later that it became clear to me what form that would take. My second child, Nicholas, was born in rather fraught circumstances, delivered by my husband on the staircase. He was – not unnaturally – the apple of his mother's eye, and maybe my predilection for purées came out of this! It is actually thanks to Nicholas that I have my career as he was the most terrible eater. He would eat yoghurt and fruit but refused almost everything else with a stubbornness that belied his tender years. Since he refused jars of baby food, I resolved to make up my own recipes to tempt him. Having always had a passion for cooking, I decided that I could easily produce foods that tasted delicious and were much better for him than the processed purées you can buy in the supermarket.

Working with Great Ormond Street Hospital, where Natasha died, I then produced my first book: *The Complete Baby and Toddler Meal Planner*, now an international bestseller, which is designed to put the joy back into feeding children. All the recipes were tested on babies and toddlers to see exactly what it was that they enjoyed eating, after all healthy food is all very well but if children don't like it then it's a wasted effort. Nicholas is now 15 years old and he and his sisters Lara (14 years old) and Scarlett (12 years old) like to cook and they eat nearly everything. They certainly keep me well in check with the views of the younger generation when it comes to culinary matters.

The power of fresh food

Home made purées have a much fresher taste than commercial jars of baby purée, which often have a shelf life of two years. I also believe that children are less likely to become fussy eaters if they are used to a good selection of fresh foods from an early age. Introducing a variety of fresh flavours at a young age will make it much easier for your child to make the transition to joining in with family meals than if your baby has been used to the uniform bland taste of commercial baby foods.

There was once a time, believe it or not, when children always ate the same food as their parents. The phenomenon of a separate diet for children consisting of chicken nuggets, burgers and chips or pizza is relatively new. This saddens me and consequently my aim has always been to find recipes that are quick and easy to prepare and can be enjoyed by everyone. Parents need not be faced with the impossible task of making separate meals for each member of the family.

This book, then, represents a collection of fine and healthy ingredients served up in an appetising way but with the 'good for you' tag placed unceremoniously around the plate. So go forth and cook to your heart's content, knowing that the content really does come from the heart.

Annabel Karmel, 2004

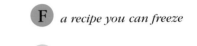

Using the recipes

In addition to the Superfoods information that stands alongside each recipe, the following symbols are used when they are relevant:

F *a recipe you can freeze*

V *suitable for vegetarians*

SuperFoods

What we feed our children today will

determine their future tomorrow.

A well-stocked larder is the best form of

preventive medicine known to man.

Eating by colour

SuperFoods are foods that have roles other than supplying the basic components of our diet – carbohydrate, protein and fat. These roles vary from boosting energy and brain power to prevention of illness and even repair of damage. Research shows that one-third of cancer cases are related to what we eat and the evidence is that fibre and fresh fruit and vegetables are in surprisingly short supply in the Western diet. Researchers estimate that diets filled with fruits and vegetables instead of fats, along with exercise, could reduce cancer incidence by 30 to 40 per cent.

So what exactly is it that makes SuperFoods so great? The answer is the chemical structures we know as vitamins, minerals and trace elements, also known collectively as phytonutrients, one of nature's many miracles. Many fruits and vegetables are packed full of these powerful natural chemicals, which have very important functions in healing and preventing illness and diseases, such as cancer and heart disease.

The incidence of cancer is increasing tremendously in Western society, as well as the incidence of obesity among children. Fruit and vegetable consumption among schoolchildren is woefully low. The latest research shows that one in five young people aged four to eighteen eat no fruit or vegetables and less than half have the recommended five portions a day. As a result, the government is introducing free fruit for school children. Eating at least five portions of fruit and vegetables per day is vital to good health and we should be incorporating fruit and vegetables into our children's diet from a very young age so they become a completely normal part of life.

Another reason for the health-giving benefits of fruit and vegetables is the presence of antioxidants. These are a group of substances that include vitamins C and E, betacarotene (the orange colour found in plants), which the body converts into vitamin A, and the minerals iron, selenium, zinc and copper. Antioxidants play a key role in protecting our bodies from the damage that can cause serious illness, particularly heart disease and cancers. Antioxidants effectively disarm certain harmful molecules known as free radicals, which can cause damage and disease. Many fruits and vegetables are rich in antioxidants and the key to making sure you are getting a good supply of antioxidants is to choose a good variety of brightly coloured fruits and vegetables to eat each day. The time to start stocking up with these protective nutrients is in childhood – it can never be too early.

The colour of food

GREEN	RED	ORANGE/YELLOW	DARK BLUE/PURPLE	WHITE
asparagus	*baked beans in*	*apricots*	*aubergine*	*apples*
avocados	*tomato sauce*	*carrots*	*beetroot*	*cauliflower*
broad beans	*cherries*	*lemon*	*blackberries*	*mushrooms*
broccoli	*grapes*	*mango*	*blackcurrants*	*onions*
brussel sprouts	*guava*	*melon (cantaloupe)*	*blueberries*	*potatoes*
cabbage	*papaya*	*oranges*	*grapes*	
kale	*plums*	*passion fruit*	*plums*	
lettuce (Cos)	*raspberries*	*peach*	*prunes*	
peas (including	*red pepper*	*pumpkin*		
mangetout)	*red/pink grapefruit*	*satsumas*		
spinach	*strawberries*	*squash*		
watercress	*tomatoes*	*swede*		
	watermelon	*sweet potatoes*		

SuperFoods by colour

It is easy to make sure children get all the SuperFoods they need, simply use the lists of fruit and vegetables given on the previous page to plan colourful meals. Fire-engine red, sunshine yellow, emerald green, rich purples – these bright fruit and vegetable colours are not just feasts for our eyes, but treasure-troves of healthy nutrients. For locked inside tomatoes, spinach, oranges and blueberries are whole sets of plant nutrients that can reduce our risk of heart disease and cancer. In general, the more colourful the food, the more nutritious it is. For example, spinach rates more highly than lettuce; the deep orange of a sweet potato contains more nutrients than an ordinary potato, and pink grapefruit is preferable to an ordinary grapefruit. It is important to ensure that you include a good variety of colours to make sure you are getting a good balance in your diet.

Green

Green foods are rich in the antioxidant vitamins A, C and E, which can protect our bodies' cells and boost our chance of living a longer, healthier life. Green leafy vegetables are also rich in iron. The green colour comes from chlorophyll, which is a plant's way of converting sunlight to energy. Studies have shown that eating broccoli regularly reduces the risk of cancer. It is also a good source of glucosinolates, which have strong anti-cancer effects by stimulating our bodies' natural defences.

Red

Lycopene is a natural pigment that gives fruits like tomatoes, red grapefruits and watermelons their red colour and is one of the most powerful cancer-fighting carotenoids. It is particularly valuable in helping to protect us from certain cancers such as prostate and cervical cancer. Carotenoids are also found in carrots, dark green vegetables, red peppers, sweet potatoes, peaches and apricots (fresh and dried), mangoes, cantaloupe melons and papayas.

Other studies have revealed that men who had high levels of lycopene in their fat stores were half as likely to have a heart

Healthy eating: *For years nutritionists have emphasised the benefits of fresh fruit and vegetables. However, lycopene is easier for our bodies to absorb when the tomatoes have been processed or cooked with a little oil in foods like tomato soup or tomato sauce for pasta and – good news – even tomato ketchup is a good source.*

attack. Most of the lycopene in the diet comes from tomatoes because of the quantity of tomatoes and tomato products we eat. However, other good sources are watermelon, guava and pink grapefruit. Lycopene is not produced by the body and needs to be derived from our diet.

Orange and yellow

Orange and yellow fruits and vegetables are high in betacarotene, the plant form of vitamin A. It is true that vitamin A improves night vision and during the Second World War it was rumoured that fighter pilots were fed a diet of carrots so they could see better in the dark. Betacarotene also protects against cancer and boosts the immune system against colds and flu. Citrus fruits are good sources of vitamin C, which is important for growth, healthy skin, healing wounds and improving the absorption of iron.

Dark blue or purple

There is lots of Vitamin C and antioxidants such as bioflavonoids and ellagic acids in blue and purple foods, which help to boost immunities against cancer. Grapes in particular contain ellagic acid. The skins of grapes also contain a substance that can lower cholesterol and prevent fats in the bloodstream from sticking together. As a result, a glass of red wine is now thought to help lower cholesterol levels.

Beetroot is especially rich in iron and magnesium. Also the pigment anthocyanin (from the Greek for 'dark blue flower') has powerful anti-cancer properties. Blueberries have one of the highest antioxidant levels of any fruit because of the high level of anthocyanins in the skin.

White

Just because you can't see it doesn't mean it isn't there. Garlic, onions and leeks contain organosulphides, which seem to stimulate the immune system and fight cancers. Organosulphides are also antioxidants. Garlic is rich in allicin, which is an antibiotic and it is antiviral.

Eating a balanced diet

To grow properly and keep healthy, children need to eat a good balanced diet. The food guide pyramid shown overleaf has been designed to show quickly the different properties of each of the food groups that make up a balanced diet and children should aim to achieve this balance by the age of five. This information is generally depicted as a pyramid to show the proportion of foods. The foods that make up the base should form the largest part of a child's diet and as the pyramid tapers towards the top, the amounts of those foods should gradually become smaller. The foods near the top should only be eaten sparingly. Children under five need a diet higher in fat and lower in fibre because of their high energy requirements.

. . . .

Did you know? *Potatoes should not be counted as a vegetable portion. A poll commissioned by the British Dietetic Association found that 81 per cent of adults would have counted potatoes as a vegetable. In fact, nutritionally they are classed as a starchy food along with bread and cereals, so your child should be eating five portions of fruit and vegetables a day on top of potatoes.*

Healthy eating: *Vitamin supplements contain only a small proportion of the nutritional benefits available from fruit and vegetables.*

Carbohydrates

This group should make up the largest part of your child's diet. Bread, cereal, rice and pasta are the body's main source of energy and also provide vitamins, minerals and fibre. Wholegrain cereals and breads are also a good source of iron. Children should eat about five servings from this group each day.

Examples of what count as one serving of carbohydrate
- **One slice of bread.**
- **A small portion of rice or pasta.**
- **A small bowl of cereal.**

Try to choose natural rather than refined carbohydrates (see page 19), such as brown rice, wholegrain bread, pulses and fruit. These foods release sugar relatively slowly into the bloodstream, which helps provide long lasting energy. Unrefined carbohydrates are also a good source of vitamins, minerals and fibre. Refined carbohydrates like white bread or white rice have lost many of their valuable nutrients during their processing. These foods still provide a good source of energy but try also to include a good proportion of natural, unrefined carbohydrates in your child's diet.

Vegetables and fruits

Vegetables and fruits are important as they provide phytochemicals such as vitamins and minerals, which help protect us against cancer and heart disease (see Eating by colour, page 10). Fruit and vegetables are also an important source of fibre. Different fruits and vegetables contain different vitamins so it is important to include as much variety as possible. Vegetables, particularly root vegetables, also provide carbohydrates for energy. For the recommended five portions a day (see page 13), a three-year-old might have a satsuma, half an apple, four dried apricots, a tablespoon of peas and a tomato throughout the day.

Dairy

These provide protein, vitamins and minerals and are the best source of calcium, which is important for good health and the formation of bones and teeth. In the first year, milk forms a very important part of your child's diet. Between the ages of one and five, children should have approximately 600 ml (20 fl oz) of milk a day or the equivalent in other dairy products. Children should have three portions of milk or dairy products each day. This could be a glass of milk, a pot of yoghurt or 30 g (1½ oz) cheese (a matchbox size).

Protein

Meat, poultry, fish, legumes, eggs and nuts supply a good source of protein, which is important for the growth, maintenance and repair of body tissue (see also Growth foods, page 17). An inadequate supply of protein can lower resistance to infection. Meat, poultry and fish also supply B vitamins, iron and zinc.

Once your baby is eating three meals a day try to make sure that she has some protein at two of these meals. Protein doesn't always have to be meat or fish; dairy products or a pulse served with a cereal are a good source. An example would be baked beans on toast. As a rough guide, children should eat meat or chicken three to four times a week and two or more portions of fish a week, one of which should be an oily variety like tuna, sardines or salmon. Protein foods like cheese or eggs are good for breakfast.

Fats and sugary processed foods

Children need proportionately more fat in their diet than adults, so for the first two years serve full-fat milk, cheese and yoghurt. Up to the age of one, children should derive 50 per cent of their energy from fat (breast milk contains 50 per cent fat). It provides a concentrated source of energy; fatty acids are important for brain and visual development (see page 17), and fats contain the fat-soluble vitamins A, D, E and K.

You should try to ensure there is enough fat in your child's diet, but you should also seek to introduce healthy eating by choosing lean meat and cutting down on fried food. Milk and cheese are good sources of fat and they are also rich in calcium, protein and vitamins. For adults and children over five, fat should provide no more than 30 per cent of their calorie intake by cutting down on junk food and processed foods like cakes and biscuits.

Vitamins and minerals

We are foolish if we think we can beat nature at its own game. Vitamin and mineral supplements can never hope to replace all the nutrients contained in food. Listed below are the main vitamins and minerals that children need to grow and be healthy.

Vitamins

Vitamins are essential for the maintenance of a healthy body. Vitamins are either water-soluble (vitamins B and C) or fat-soluble (A, D, E and K). Water-soluble vitamins, except for vitamin B12, cannot be stored in the body, so foods containing these should be eaten regularly. These vitamins are destroyed by heat and dissolve in water, so do not overcook foods that contain them. Fat-soluble vitamins can be stored in the body and excessive amounts accumulate and can be toxic. If a balanced diet is eaten it is highly unlikely that this would happen, but beware of supplements.

Vitamin A: Also known as retinol, vitamin A only occurs in animal foods but fruit and vegetables contain carotenoids, which are converted to vitamin A by our bodies. Important for growth, preventing infections of the nose, throat and lungs, healthy skin and good night vision, vitamin A is found in liver, oily fish, full-fat milk and cheese, butter, margarine and egg yolks.

The food pyramid

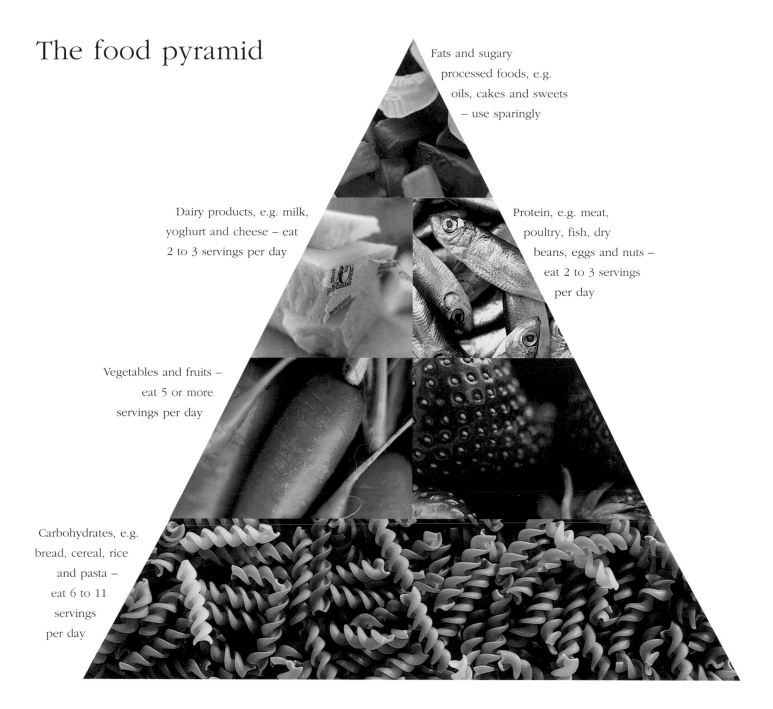

Fats and sugary processed foods, e.g. oils, cakes and sweets – use sparingly

Dairy products, e.g. milk, yoghurt and cheese – eat 2 to 3 servings per day

Protein, e.g. meat, poultry, fish, dry beans, eggs and nuts – eat 2 to 3 servings per day

Vegetables and fruits – eat 5 or more servings per day

Carbohydrates, e.g. bread, cereal, rice and pasta – eat 6 to 11 servings per day

A balanced diet for adults and children over five years old should contain approximately 20% protein, 35% fat and 45% carbohydrates. Children under five years of age need a diet higher in fat and lower in fibre, but gradually their diet will change to become more in line with an adult diet.

B complex vitamins: These are important for growth, the development of a healthy nervous system and are essential for converting food into energy. No foods except liver and brewers' yeast extract contain all of the vitamins in the B group. Good sources are meat, dairy produce, eggs, sardines, dark green leafy vegetables, wholegrain cereals, tofu, nuts, yeast extract (not suitable for infants as preparations are often very high in sodium), and bananas.

Vitamin C: This vitamin cannot be produced by our bodies and is needed for the growth and repair of body tissues, healthy skin and the healing of wounds. It is also important because it helps the body absorb iron and is a powerful antioxidant. Good sources are citrus fruits, strawberries, kiwi fruit, blackcurrants, sweet peppers, broccoli, dark green leafy vegetables and peppers.

Vitamin D: Although this is found in a few foods it is mainly manufactured by the skin when it is exposed to sunlight. This is one of the reasons why children should try to get some fresh air every day. It is needed to absorb calcium and phosphorus for healthy bones and teeth and to avoid rickets. Good sources are oily fish such as tuna, salmon and sardines, milk and dairy products, eggs and margarine.

Vitamin E: This is needed to help develop and maintain strong cells, protect against heart disease and maintain good function in the nervous system, and it may be important in maintaining immunity. Good sources for vitamin E are vegetable oil, wheatgerm, avocado, nuts and seeds.

Vitamin supplements: *The Department of Health recommends giving a vitamin supplement of A, C*

and D from the age of 6 months if your baby is being breastfed or is drinking less than 500 ml (18 fl oz) of infant formula a day. Ask your health centre or baby clinic for advice.

Minerals

There are many minerals in food and of these, iron and zinc are very important. Selenium and copper are also essential to a well-rounded diet: they are both antioxidants, which means they help prevent damage to cells from free radicals (see page 10). Good sources for selenium include wholegrains, nuts, meat, poultry and fish and good sources of copper are wholegrain cereals, bread and pasta, and dried fruit, tofu, pulses, nuts and seeds.

Iron: Iron deficiency is the commonest nutritional deficiency in the Western world. Babies are born with a store of iron that lasts for about the first six months. When this in-built store of iron is depleted, a baby must obtain sufficient iron from the diet. There are a few types of iron, the best source of which is found in meat and is easily absorbed by the body. Plant food sources are more difficult to absorb and the third type, added by manufacturers to foods such as breakfast cereals, is absorbed less well. However, if foods or drinks containing vitamin C are eaten at the same meal, then the iron is better absorbed. Offer fresh fruits like kiwis, citrus or berry fruits for dessert or a small glass of pure fruit juice. A good combination for breakfast would be an iron-fortified cereal followed by kiwi fruit and strawberries.

Zinc: In general, dark red meat has a higher zinc content than white meat and fish has less than meat. Cereals are a good source of zinc but as it is contained in the outer layer of the grain, the more refined the cereal, the less zinc there is. Good sources include red meat, wholemeal bread, Cheddar cheese, lentils, shellfish, pumpkin seeds and fortified breakfast cereals.

Growth foods

Children grow and develop rapidly. Protein is the building block of all the cells in our bodies and therefore an essential part of the diet. Since children grow so quickly, they have a higher requirement for protein than do adults. As well as helping growth, proteins are also important for repairing any damage to body tissue. It is reassuring to know that protein deficiency is almost unheard of in this country and most of us eat more protein than we need.

Protein is made up of amino acids, some of which the body can manufacture and some of which can be obtained from food. Animal proteins contain all the amino acids that the body needs, whereas soya is the only plant-based food that contains all the essential amino acids. To provide complete proteins, pulses and grains need to be combined, such as baked beans on toast or lentils and rice. Good animal sources of protein are red meat, poultry, fish, eggs, milk, cheese, grains, pulses and tofu.

Fats and oils

Fats and oils are also included in this group of growth foods, not for their essential fatty acid properties but for their high caloric contents. Fats are like liquid gold packed full of energy. In order to meet the high demands for energy of a growing infant or child, the diet must contain adequate amounts of fat.

Babies and young children need more fat in their diet than adults because of their rapid growth, so don't be worried about adding a good dollop of butter to a baked potato or making pasta in a creamy cheese sauce.

Brain foods

Eggs are rich in choline, a B vitamin that is a key component in the

....

Did you know? *Research suggests that a diet rich in omega-6 and omega-3 acids may improve the performance of children with attention deficit disorder, hyperactivity or dyspraxia.*

brain transmitter 'acetyl choline' which is crucial for memory. There are many important factors in brain development but no scientifically proven links with specific types of food. That said, a balanced and varied diet and a good breakfast obviously ensures that all possible factors important for brain development are present and there are some foods that are better than others for stimulating the brain cells.

Natural starches

Although weighing only 2 per cent of total body weight, the brain uses approximately 20 per cent of the body's energy at rest. The brain's energy stores are very small, so to keep it functioning at its best it needs sugar or fuel, which is derived from carbohydrates. When levels of sugar in the blood fluctuate, behaviour and learning become erratic. The best foods to keep blood sugars steady for the brain are the complex carbohydrates that contain natural starches (see page 19) and so supply a steady source of fuel, such as porridge, wholegrain cereal, brown rice and sweet potatoes.

Iron

Foods that contain iron have been shown to prevent anaemia, a condition that leads to tiredness, decreased mental alertness, lowered IQ and overall apathy. Iron is also important for transporting oxygen in haemoglobin in our red blood cells to all organs in the body including our brain, therefore iron is vital for good brain function. High iron foods are red meat, liver, dried fruit and iron-enriched cereals such as Weetabix.

Fatty acids

In the first year of life, a baby's brain grows at a very fast rate, generally tripling in size by the first birthday. Fats are a major component of the brain – this is one of the reasons why 50 per cent of the calories of breast milk are composed of fat.

Oily fish like salmon, mackerel, tuna and sardines are good brain boosters. This is due to their high levels of omega-3 essential fats which optimise messaging between nerve cells in the brain. Good intakes are crucial for normal brain functioning in children

and can sometimes improve problems like dyslexia and hyperactivity. There are two essential types of fatty acids that have been shown to be important for brain and visual development. They are alpha-linolenic (omega-3) and linoleic (omega-6) acids.

Foods rich in omega-3 are linseed oil, walnut oil, salmon, tuna, trout and sardines. Foods rich in omega-6 are safflower oil, grapeseed oil, sunflower oil and soft polyunsaturated margarine. Some foods are fortified with omega-3 oils, like certain spreads, Columbus eggs and some breads.

Energy-boosting foods

Foods containing carbohydrates are the main providers of energy in the diet. There are two types of carbohydrates: sugars (simple carbohydrates) and starches (complex carbohydrates), each of which can be found in two forms: natural or refined.

- Natural sugars are found in fruits and fruit juices.
- Refined sugars, including white and brown sugar and honey, are found in cakes, biscuits, jelly and soft drinks.
- Natural starches are found in wholegrain and wholemeal breakfast cereals, wholemeal flour and bread, brown rice, potatoes, porridge oats, lentils, bananas and root vegetables.
- Refined starches are found in white flour and white bread, sugary processed breakfast cereals, white rice, white pasta, biscuits and cakes.

All carbohydrates taken in by the body have to be digested and converted into glucose – a type of sugar. Of these, the natural carbohydrates provide the best source of energy as they keep blood sugar levels constant because they release their sugar

Healthy eating: *It is best to wash fruit but leave the skin on fruits like apples or peaches, as a lot of the nutrients lie just below the skin.*

Healthy eating: *If your child needs energy for a football match or sports day, it is best to give a meal based on foods that release sugar slowly into the bloodstream such as brown rice, pasta, wholegrain cereals, vegetables and fruit. A good snack might be peanut butter sandwiches on wholegrain bread or a banana. Give water or pure fruit juice instead of soft drinks. The sugar in soft drinks could trigger low blood sugar, leaving your child feeling tired. After physical activity and particularly in hot weather don't let your child wait until he feels thirsty to give him a drink. The chances are that he will already be dehydrated.*

content into the bloodstream slowly, thus giving long-lasting energy. They also retain their vitamins, minerals and fibre, so try to include some wholegrain versions like brown rice and wholemeal bread in the diet.

Starchy foods like potato, rice, pasta or bread provide energy at a slower rate than sugary foods. Refined sugars are quickly absorbed by the body, so energy levels rise dramatically for a short while. However, the problem is that the pancreas then produces lots of insulin in a bid to break down the sugar, which can lead to a rapid decline in energy. Fruit sugars provide quick energy but do not cause such a rapid rise and fall in energy because the fibre slows the absorption of the sugars.

The consumption of high-sugar foods and drinks like biscuits, cakes and soft drinks causes a rapid rise in blood sugar that can result in the body over compensating, which leads to a dip in blood sugar levels, resulting in low levels of physical and mental energy. Instead, for sustained energy it is much better to choose fresh fruit, nuts and seeds, rice cakes or nutritious sandwiches made with wholemeal bread. With these foods in your diet, your energy levels will remain far more consistent and your concentration on a more even keel.

A good vegetarian diet

More and more families with children are choosing to become vegetarian and a balanced vegetarian diet can be very healthy. However, it is important not to give up meat without replacing the nutrients that meat provides, particularly protein, iron, zinc and possibly some B vitamins.

Adult and children's diets do not always follow the same guidelines and whereas a fairly bulky high-fibre vegetarian diet might suit adults, it is not suitable for young children who are growing as it can replace more energy-dense foods such as fat and carbohydrate. Also a lot of fibre in the diet can inhibit the absorption of minerals such as zinc, iron and calcium and is very bulky and filling and can even cause toddler diarrhoea.

Bringing up a baby on a vegetarian diet with a good volume of either breast milk or infant formula can provide all the nutrients they need.

The importance of protein

Protein supplies your child with amino acids, essential chemicals which are the body's building blocks. Whilst all animal proteins including egg and dairy products provide a high quality protein containing all the essential amino acids, cereals and vegetable proteins (e.g. peas, beans, lentils, and nuts and seeds) have a lower quality. Soya is the only plant-based food that contains all the amino acids.

To ensure your child gets a high quality protein at each meal try to combine a cereal food, e.g. pasta, bread or rice, together with eggs, dairy products like cheese, pulses or nuts. Good ideas are baked beans on toast, lentil soup with a wholegrain roll, peanut butter sandwiches, baked potato with cheese and milk and pasta with cheese sauce. Good vegetarian sources of protein include eggs, milk, cheese, yoghurt, soya, beans, lentils, nuts and seeds.

Examples of good protein combinations

- A cereal food such as pasta, bread or rice with eggs, cheese, pulses or nuts.
- Baked beans on toast.
- Baked potato with cheese and milk.
- Pasta with cheese sauce.

The importance of iron

It is important to make sure that children brought up on a vegetarian diet have an adequate supply of iron (see page 17). Good vegetarian sources of iron include fortified breakfast cereals, egg yolk, wholemeal bread and beans and lentils, dark green leafy vegetables and dried fruit, especially apricots and peaches. Iron is absorbed more efficiently by the body if combined with vitamin C so offer a food or drink high in vitamin C at each meal.

The importance of calcium

Calcium is important for the health and formation of bones and teeth and to begin with breast or formula milk contains all the calcium that your baby needs. However, from six months you can introduce cow's milk and dairy products as a food (see pages 28, 68 and 92). Other good vegetarian sources of calcium are tofu (calcium fortified), dried figs and apricots, nuts, sesame seeds and hummus, tinned sardines and fortified soya milk.

B vitamins

Vitamin B12 is needed for growth and division of cells. It is only found in foods of animal origin such as meat, poultry, fish, eggs and dairy produce. Some breakfast cereals are also fortified with vitamin B12 and yeast extract is another source. Vegetarians can obtain sufficient vitamin B12 from eggs and dairy produce.

Vegan diet

If you plan to follow a vegan diet you should plan your child's diet carefully, in consultation with a paediatric dietitian (contact the British Dietetic Association for more information).

Shopping for food

All foods and their ingredients must be safe by law. When looking at labels do not be misled into thinking that all E numbers are bad – for example, E162 is the natural red colouring from beetroot juice. When there is an 'E' prefix before an additive, this means that it is permitted throughout the EU and has passed safety testing.

However, some food additives may cause problems in a small percentage of children who are sensitive to them. For example, the additives listed below are quite commonly found in children's junk food and were banned in countries such as Norway and Denmark, but when they joined the EC the ban was lifted.

Tartrazine	E102	Yellow Food Colouring
Sunset Yellow	E110	Orangey-yellow Food Colouring
Carmoisine	E122	Red Food Colouring
Ponceau 4R	E124	Red Food Colouring
Sodium Benzoate	E211	Preservative

Food labels list ingredients in order of decreasing weight. Try to choose foods that are low in sugar, salt and saturated fat and avoid large amounts of colourings and artificial flavourings.

What is a little and what is a lot:

per 100 g of food	high	low
SUGAR	10 g	2 g
FAT	20 g	3 g
SATURATES	5 g	1 g
FIBRE	3 g	0.5 g
SODIUM	0.5 g	0.1 g

Fat and fibre

The amount of fat and fibre is not really an issue as children of this age need a more nutrient-dense diet with more fat and less fibre. However, from two years upwards, children should gradually move towards an adult-type diet (see the food pyramid on page 15). When looking at labels, it is useful to check that the amount of saturates is not a large percentage of the total fat. There are two main types of fat: saturated fat derived mainly from animal sources, e.g. butter, lard and the fat in meat and dairy produce; and unsaturated fat, e.g. vegetable oil. As a general rule vegetable fats are healthier than animal fats with the exception of fish oils in fish like salmon and sardines.

Salt

Too much salt in the diet may contribute to high blood pressure, which can increase the risk of a stroke, coronary heart disease and kidney disease. It is therefore a good idea for the whole family to become accustomed to less salt in the diet. Try not to add too much salt while cooking and avoid salt on the table.

Babies under one year should not have any salt added to their food as a baby's kidneys are too immature to cope with added salt. Toddlers (age 1 to 3) should have no more than 2 g of salt (about one third of a teaspoon) per day and a 4- to 6-year-old should have no more than 3 g of salt a day. Three quarters of the salt we eat comes from processed foods like pot noodles, sausages and burgers, pizzas, spaghetti hoops and crisps.

Sugar

Labels often break carbohydrates into starch and sugars and it is useful to know that 5 g of sugar makes one teaspoon. However, in many cases, because of poor labelling, it is impossible to establish the sugar content of sweet foods. Beware: many foods marketed for children like breakfast cereals and cereal bars may contain more than 35 per cent sugar.

Sugar may come in many disguises such as sucrose, glucose, glucose syrup, maltose, dextrose, fructose, golden syrup, honey and fruit juices. And manufacturers can hide the amount of sugar in a product by using three different types of sugar, e.g. sugar, corn syrup and honey, and by listing each sugar separately. Each appears lower down the list, making it more difficult to judge the total amount of sugar in the product. The term 'No added sugar' can also be misleading, for the product could still contain honey, glucose, corn syrup and concentrated apple juice, which are just as harmful to your child's teeth.

Most soft drinks are packed with sugar. A can of Coke or similar fizzy drink can contain 35 to 40 g (1¼-1½ oz) sugar, which is equivalent to about eight teaspoons. Take care when choosing fruit juices as pure unsweetened juices should contain no added sugars except the 15 g (½ oz) per litre that manufacturers are allowed. There are some individual cartons of fruit juice on the market that contain 25 g (1 oz) of sugar, which represents more than seven teaspoons of sugar, and even fruit sugars will cause tooth decay. Likewise, watch out for juice drinks, which can contain as little as 5 per cent juice.

Yoghurts and fromage frais are a good source of calcium but some fromage frais can contain as many as four sugar lumps. Despite their healthy image, many yoghurts contain a lot of added sugar, thickeners, colours and flavourings. Similarly, many breakfast cereals designed to appeal to children can contain as much as 50 per cent sugar. It would be much better for your child to start the day with a good old-fashioned cereal like porridge or muesli, even if your child adds honey or a little sugar.

Foods and drinks for babies and young children are not allowed to contain artificial sweeteners. However, these are included in many foods specifically targeted at youngsters including soft drinks, yoghurts and ice lollies 'disguised' as technical jargon. When doing the weekly shop, look carefully at the ingredients of what you are buying and beware if they contain acesulfame k, aspartame, saccharin or sorbitol, these are, in fact, artificial sweeteners.

Frozen food

In some cases, processed foods actually retain more nutrients than the unprocessed form. Perhaps the best example of this is frozen vegetables and fruits, which are picked and frozen within hours of harvest, thus locking in valuable nutrients. Fresh vegetables and fruits may have been stored for long periods before purchase or use and the longer they remain on the shelf or in cold storage the more nutrients they lose. However, research has shown that frozen vegetables and fruits are just as good – if not better – for you as their fresh relations.

Healthy eating: *Manufacturers add vitamins and minerals to a variety of foods aimed at children, from sugary refined breakfast cereals to tinned pasta and ice lollies. It is a mistake to believe that adding vitamins to an otherwise unhealthy food will make it healthy, but sadly for a large percentage of children this source of vitamins, calcium and iron is very important.*

Keep a good supply of frozen fruit and vegetables such as frozen peas, spinach, sweetcorn, summer berries and thick-cut oven chips in stock in your deep freeze. They make good standbys, they don't go mouldy, they are quick and easy to prepare and inexpensive.

Canned food

The process of canning preserves food by heating it to a sufficiently high temperature and replacing the oxygen with inactive gasses and then sealing it in an airtight container to prevent microbial contamination. Most canned foods will keep for one year and they retain many nutrients, including protein and vitamins A and D and riboflavin.

The high temperatures involved in canning tend to destroy vitamin B1 and vitamin C in vegetables and savoury foods. But canned fruit and fruit juices tend to retain most of their vitamins. Most acidic foods retain their vitamin C content so canned tomatoes are still good for you. Be aware that foods canned in brine are high in salt. Fruits canned in syrup are high in sugar, so instead choose fruits canned in natural juice.

Convenience food

Whereas many chilled convenience meals are high in salt and fat, there are quite a number of convenience foods that are good to store in your larder (see the suggestions that are given overleaf).

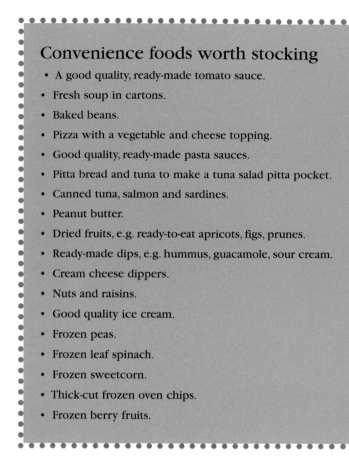

Convenience foods worth stocking

- A good quality, ready-made tomato sauce.
- Fresh soup in cartons.
- Baked beans.
- Pizza with a vegetable and cheese topping.
- Good quality, ready-made pasta sauces.
- Pitta bread and tuna to make a tuna salad pitta pocket.
- Canned tuna, salmon and sardines.
- Peanut butter.
- Dried fruits, e.g. ready-to-eat apricots, figs, prunes.
- Ready-made dips, e.g. hummus, guacamole, sour cream.
- Cream cheese dippers.
- Nuts and raisins.
- Good quality ice cream.
- Frozen peas.
- Frozen leaf spinach.
- Frozen sweetcorn.
- Thick-cut frozen oven chips.
- Frozen berry fruits.

Organic foods

Organic baby foods have grown in popularity as people have become increasingly concerned about the effects of pesticides and other agricultural chemicals on children's health. Organic farming is an environmentally friendly option, but it generates higher prices and parents should not feel that a non-organic diet is unhealthy. The risk of not including fruits and vegetables in children's diets are far greater and there is no scientific evidence that pesticide levels in ordinary fruit and vegetables are harmful to babies and young children.

Organic food is grown in soil without the use of artificial fertilisers or pesticides and instead uses traditional crop rotation where possible and makes the most of natural fertilisers. Animals are reared without the routine use of antibiotics, growth hormones or worm injections. The animals reared must also be allowed to live natural, contented lives. However, pesticides have been used for so many years that they may still be present in the soil, water and air. Spray drift of chemicals from neighbouring farms make it impossible to guarantee that organic food is free from pesticide residues.

There is no law – and it is unlikely to occur – to say that organic produce must taste better. If you choose to go organic, you will need to shop at least two or three times a week as there are no chemical preservatives in organic food, and fruit and vegetables in particular will detiorate more quickly.

GM foods: are these the new SuperFoods?

There is a great deal of controversy about the introduction of genetically modified (GM) crops and foods. Genetically engineering food is a new way of producing foods by taking DNA from one species and inserting it into another. One benefit of this would be that genetic modification could be used to enhance the protein content of rice – the lack of protein is a major cause of illness in many third-world countries.

Unlike conventional breeding, where genes can only be transferred between plants or animals of the same or closely related species, genetic engineering also enables genes to be transferred between different species and potentially even between animals and plants. For example, work is under way to produce plants with an in-built mechanism to fight frost damage. One possibility would involve utilising the genes in fish, which enable them to tolerate extreme cold.

If you want to avoid foods containing GM material, check the labelling carefully. European law rules that all ingredients that contain or consist of GM organisms must be listed. Also, products such as meat or milk that come from animals fed on GM feed must be clearly labelled.

Many people are worried that the long-term effects of eating genetically modified food are as yet unknown and could be harmful to the environment.

6 months:
the best first foods for your baby

Weaning your baby is an exciting time for both of you. It's a huge step forward for your baby into a whole new world of tastes and textures.

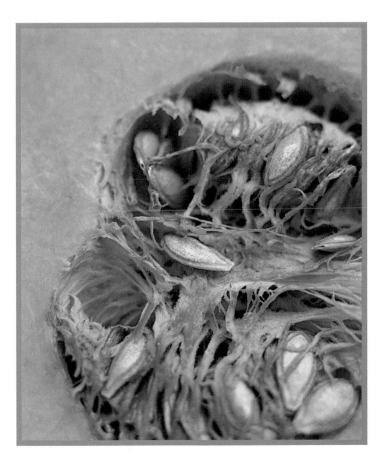

Breastfeeding benefits

For the first six months of life, babies need nothing more than milk as this provides all the energy and nutrients that they need. Breast milk contains particular proteins called antibodies and white blood cells, which help to protect a baby from infection. Breast milk is also rich in the omega-3 essential fatty acids that are important for brain development. There is also evidence that breastfeeding for thirteen weeks or more reduces the incidence of gastroenteritis and respiratory infections. Breastfeeding has also been shown to delay the onset and reduce the severity of allergies in children from families with a history of asthma, hayfever, eczema and food allergies. The colostrum that a mother produces in the first few days of breastfeeding is a very important source of antibodies, so there is a benefit in breastfeeding even for a short period. For a mother the benefits of breastfeeding include a lower risk of ovarian cancer and breast cancer. Furthermore, a baby's suckling at the breast causes the uterus to contract so that it returns to its normal size much faster.

Healthy eating: *Infant formula has similar amounts of nutrients, minerals and vitamins to breast milk but none of the properties breast milk has to protect against infection. In breast milk, the amount of minerals available such as iron and zinc is excellent.*

How much milk?

Between 4 and 6 months, babies should have between 600 and 800 ml (21 and 28 fl oz) of milk a day and from the age of six months to one year, babies should have between 500 and 800 ml (17 and 28 fl oz) of milk each day, mostly in the form of breast milk or formula milk. Whilst you can use cow's milk in cooking and with breakfast cereals, breast milk or formula should remain your baby's main drink as these contain nutrients that cow's milk

Daily milk consumption

APPROXIMATE AGE	NUMBER OF FEEDS/DAY
1 to 2 weeks	7 to 8
2 to 6 weeks	6 to 7
2 months	5 to 6
3 months	5
6 months	4

lacks, such as iron and vitamin C. Do not fill up your baby with solid foods at the expense of milk. Avoid baby drinks such as juices as the only fluid your baby needs is milk. If the weather is very hot and you feel your baby needs extra fluid, offer boiled, cooled water. There is extra fluid in the food your baby is eating because purées have a high water content.

What milk?

Cow's, goat's, sheep's, soya (non-infant, carton), rice and oats milks are not suitable as your baby's main drink before one year as they do not contain enough iron and other nutrients for proper growth. Whole cow's milk can be used in cooking or with cereal from six months but should not be given as your baby's main drink before the age of one year.

Young babies have high energy and nutrient requirements so skimmed milk should not be introduced before five years because it is very low in energy. However, semi-skimmed milk can be given from the age of two if your child is eating and growing well.

Follow-on formula has higher levels of iron, vitamin D, protein and sodium than infant formulas. It should only be given from six months of age. Follow-on milks are not intended to replace breast milk or regular infant formulas, which are suitable up to twelve months of age. However, follow-on milks are nutritionally more suitable than cow's milk and are generally recommended for children who are at risk of iron deficiency. Follow-on milks may be used until 24 months of age.

Other drinks for your baby

The only drink apart from breast or formula milk that your baby should have in the first six months is water. Boiled, cooled tap water is best. Bottled mineral water can contain high concentrations of mineral salts, which are unsuitable for young babies. High levels of nitrates, sulphates and fluoride should be avoided. Carbonated (fizzy) water is also unsuitable for babies.

Specially manufactured fruit and herbal drinks for babies can sometimes contain quite large amounts of sugar, which can lead to tooth decay. If you want to give your baby fruit juice, it is much better to squeeze your own or choose one that contains only natural fruit sugars. Orange juice is a good source of vitamin C, which will help your child to absorb iron. All fruit juices should be diluted five parts water to one part juice as even natural fruit sugars can cause tooth decay. Try to confine drinks other than water or milk to mealtimes; fruit or herbal drinks can take away a young baby's appetite from more valuable foods and milk at mealtimes.

Introducing solids

The UK Department of Health guidelines recommend exclusive breastfeeding if possible for the first 6 months as this should meet all your baby's nutritional needs. Babies given formula milk should also delay weaning onto solids until 6 months. A very young baby's digestive and immune system is not sufficiently developed before this time and there is a greater risk of food allergy occurring.

While sucking is a natural reflex, babies need to be ready to learn the new skill of pushing food to the back of the mouth with their tongues and swallowing. To eat from a spoon your baby has to be able to use his tongue to push food back, rather than forward, in his mouth and to be able to use his lips to pull food off the spoon. Until now he's only been used to using his jaw and cheek muscles for sucking in his milk, so this is a completely new experience.

Never leave a baby or toddler alone with food as he may choke (see page 69 for what to do if this happens). If weaning is delayed until after six months, some babies can have difficulty learning to swallow and chew food.

Signs that your baby is ready for solids
• He is still hungry after a full milk feed.
• He starts waking more during the night demanding to be fed.
• He demands feeds more often.

The best first foods for your baby

The first foods that you give your baby must be easy to digest and unlikely to provoke an allergic reaction. Don't be tempted to add salt or sugar to your baby's food, however bland. Salt may harm your baby's kidneys and sugar will encourage a sweet tooth.

For the first few weeks it is not a good idea to give mixtures of foods other than baby rice mixed with a fruit or vegetable purée. Weaning is a good time to discover if there are any foods that your baby does not tolerate well, and when foods are mixed together it is hard to tell which of them is causing a problem.

First vegetables: Carrot, potato, swede, parsnip, pumpkin, butternut squash (pumpkin) and sweet potato (see pages 36 to 39). Root vegetables like carrots and sweet potato tend to be the most popular with very young babies as they are sweet and smooth once puréed. After first tastes, you can start to introduce other vegetables like courgette (zucchini), cauliflower, broccoli and peas.

First fruits: Apple, pear, banana, papaya (pawpaw) and avocado (see pages 40 to 42).

Baby rice: Mixed with water, breast or formula milk, baby rice is easily digested and its milky taste makes an easy transition to solids. Choose one that is sugar free. Baby rice combines well with both fruit and vegetable purées.

Meat: Puréed chicken, turkey or beef can be included in a baby's diet and are good sources of iron. It's a good idea to combine them with root vegetables as this helps to produce a texture that is much smoother and easier to swallow.

Fish: Introduce soft white fish – plaice or cod is ideal.

Foods to avoid

• Salt: Babies under a year should not have any salt added to their food as this can strain immature kidneys and cause dehydration. A preference for salt can become established at an early age and eating too much salt may lead to high blood pressure later in life. Also avoid smoked foods.

• Sugar: Unless food is really tart, don't add sugar. Adding sugar is habit-forming and increases the risk of tooth decay.

• Foods containing gluten: i.e. wheat, oats, barley and rye, should not be introduced before 6 months. When buying baby cereals and rusks before 6 months make sure they are gluten-free. Baby rice is the safest to try at first.

• Raw or lightly cooked eggs: Eggs should not be given before 6 months (due to the risk of salmonella infection) and should be cooked until the yolk and white are solid.

• Unpasteurised cheeses: e.g. Brie, Camembert or Danish Blue before 12 months due to the risk of listeria infection.

• Shellfish: Should not be given until at least 1 year old due to the risk of food poisoning and potential allergy.

• Nuts: Chopped and whole nuts are not recommended before the age of 5 due to the risk of choking. There is also a risk of allergic reaction to nuts.

• Honey: Should not be given before one year. It can very occasionally contain a type of bacteria that can result in a potentially serious illness called 'infant botulism'.

When to give feeds

Try to make feeding a special time to share with your baby rather than a chore and pick a time of day when you are not rushed or liable to be distracted. If possible, try to feed your baby around the same time every day to establish some kind of routine. Babies are used to food coming in a non-stop steady stream and sometimes find the gaps between spoonfuls annoying. For some babies, it may be a good idea to begin by giving a little milk before their solids so that they are not frantically hungry, or they may become frustrated. For the first few days a baby will probably only have a tiny amount – maybe one or two spoonfuls. Start with one feed a day, probably around lunchtime, and gradually increase to about three feeds a day (breakfast, lunch and supper) by five or six months (see my meal planners on pages 33 to 35). Always test the temperature of your food before giving it to your baby. Sit your baby on your lap or in a baby chair and try to make it an enjoyable experience by smiling and talking to your baby as you feed her.

Food rejection

Avoid making a fuss if your baby won't eat and try to stay relaxed. Try re-introducing food after a couple of days if at first solids are refused, or prepare a runnier purée so that it is easier for your baby to swallow. You could also try dipping a clean finger in the purée and allowing your baby to suck it off your finger as some babies don't like the feel of a spoon in their mouths to begin with. If your baby only takes a very little food, try not to make mealtimes too drawn out in an attempt to get him to eat more. Babies usually know when they have had enough.

Making baby food

By making baby food yourself, you can be sure of using only the best quality ingredients without the need for thickeners or additives. It also works out much cheaper to make baby food at home rather than buying commercial brands. Introducing a wide range of foods is important in establishing a varied and healthy diet and you can make up your own combinations to suit your baby. You have the choice of organic fruit and vegetables if you like (see page 24).

Judging quantities

It is difficult to predict how much a baby will eat since all babies' appetites and needs are different. As a very rough guide you will probably find that at the beginning your baby will only take one or two tablespoons of purée from a small, shallow weaning spoon so allow about two tablespoon ice-cube portions. As your baby develops, probably the best advice is to offer your baby 5–6 tablespoons of purée and keep going until her interest starts to wane. Provided your baby is gaining weight and has plenty of energy you can rest assured that she is doing fine. If your baby has an insatiable appetite and you are worried that she is overweight, then seek professional advice.

Texture

To begin with, purées should be quite runny, resembling the consistency of a thick soup, and made up of only one or two ingredients. Your baby's purées should not be made up with tap water that has not been boiled but only with the water from the bottom of the steamer or the cooking liquid if boiling vegetables in a saucepan. You can thin purées by adding extra cooking liquid or milk and thicken purées by stirring in a little baby rice.

What temperature?

A baby's mouth is more sensitive to heat than ours and food should be given at room temperature or lukewarm. If re-heating in a microwave, heat until piping hot all the way through, allow to cool, then stir thoroughly to get rid of any hot spots and check the temperature before giving it to your baby.

Hygiene

Very young babies are particularly vulnerable to the effects of food poisoning so you should take great care in the storage and preparation of your baby's food. Warm milk is the perfect breeding ground for bacteria, so scrupulously wash and sterilise bottles, teats and feeding cup spouts for the first year. Weaning spoons should be sterilised for the first nine months. However, once your baby is crawling around and exploring objects in his mouth, there is little point in sterilising anything other than bottles and teats. Your baby's bowls can be washed in a dishwasher but should be wiped with a clean tea towel. The most popular methods of sterilising are a microwave or steam steriliser or tablets or solution.

Equipment

Bibs: Weaning can be a very messy business so arm yourself with a selection of bibs. Bibs with sleeves give good protection, wipe-clean bibs save on the washing and plastic pelican bibs with a trough are suitable for older children.

Bouncy chair: A small bouncy chair that supports your baby's back is ideal for the first stages of weaning.

Ice-cube trays or mini-freezer pots: These allow you to prepare baby purées in bulk and freeze extra portions so that you only need to cook for your baby once or twice a week.

Steamer: Steaming food is one of the best ways to preserve nutrient. A multi-layered steamer is useful as it allows you to cook several foods simultaneously.

Weaning bowls: Buy a selection of small, heatproof weaning bowls.

Weaning spoon: A baby's gums are sensitive so instead of using a hard metal spoon, feed her with a small plastic weaning spoon. It should be shallow with no sharp edges.

Electric hand-held blender: This is easy to clean and ideal for making small quantities of baby purées.

Food processor: This is good for puréeing larger quantities when making batches of purées for freezing. Many have a mini-bowl attachment, which will work better with smaller quantities.

Mini-processors: These are useful for making small quantities of a baby purée.

Mouli: This is a hand-turned food mill that is ideal for foods that have a tough skin like peas or dried apricots as you can produce a smooth purée and hold back any indigestible husks or skins. Puréeing potato in a food processor tends to break down the starches and produces a sticky, glutinous pulp so potato is much better puréed using a mouli.

Methods of cooking

Boiling: Use the minimum amount of water and be careful not to overcook the vegetables and fruits. Add enough of the cooking liquid to make a smooth purée.

Microwaving: Chop the vegetables or fruit and put in a suitable dish. Add a little water, cover leaving an air vent and cook on full power until tender. Purée to the desired consistency but take care to stir well and check that it is not too hot to serve to your baby.

Steaming: This is the best way to preserve the fresh taste and vitamins in vegetables and fruits. Vitamins B and C are water-soluble and can easily be destroyed by overcooking, especially when fruits and vegetables are boiled in water.

Freezing

You will find that if you try to make very small portions of baby purées, it will be difficult to blend them to a very smooth texture. So it is much less time consuming to prepare your baby's food in batches and freeze individual portions in ice-cube trays or small freezer containers. Freeze the food as soon as it has cooled down. Baby foods can be stored in the freezer for up to 6 weeks.

Thaw foods by either taking them out of the freezer several hours before a meal, heating gently in a saucepan or defrosting in a microwave. Always re-heat foods thoroughly, allow to cool and test the temperature before giving the food to your baby. If re-heating in a microwave, ensure that you stir the food to get rid of any hot spots.

Never re-freeze meals that have already been frozen and do not re-heat foods more than once. However, commercially frozen foods like frozen peas can be re-frozen once they have been cooked.

The importance of iron

Iron is very important for your baby's physical and mental development. A baby is born with a store of iron that lasts for about the first 6 months. After this it is important that your baby gets the iron he needs from his diet. Iron deficiency is the most common nutritional deficiency in young children. Surveys have shown that one in every five babies aged 10 to 12 months has daily intakes of iron below the recommended level. Iron deficiency can cause your child to feel tired, run down and more prone to infection. Between 6 months and 2 years is a critical time for brain development and a lack of iron in the diet can lead to impaired mental development.

How to spot iron deficiency

Iron deficiency can be hard to detect. Your baby may seem pale and tired; she may also seem more prone to infection. Iron deficiency may lead to anaemia, which can result in irritability, loss of appetite and can impair your baby's growth and development.

Good sources of iron: *Red meat, particularly liver; Chicken or turkey (especially the dark meat); Oily fish (canned sardines, salmon, mackerel, fresh tuna); Pulses (lentils, baked beans); Iron-fortified breakfast cereals; Bread; Egg yolk; Green vegetables (spinach, broccoli); Dried fruit (especially apricots).*

Tip *Iron in foods of animal origin like red meat or poultry is much better absorbed than iron in foods of plant origin. Vitamin C also helps boost iron absorption.*

Meal planners

In this and the following chapters I have devised meal planners that will help you through weaning. Every baby develops at his own pace so these should be used as a guide since there are many variations on the foods that can be given and the order in which they can be introduced.

I have tried to give as wide a choice of recipes as possible, although I know that in practice, meals that your baby enjoys will be repeated many times and there is nothing wrong with giving the same food on two consecutive days – it is also a more practical proposition. Adapt the recipes according to seasonal fruits and vegetables.

From weaning: weeks 1 and 2

	BREAKFAST	MID-MORNING	LUNCH	MID-AFTERNOON	SUPPER	BEDTIME
DAY 1	*Breast or formula milk*	*Breast or formula milk*	*Milk 3 tsp baby rice mixed with milk*	*Breast or formula milk*	*Breast or formula milk*	*Breast or formula milk*
DAY 2	*Breast or formula milk*	*Breast or formula milk*	*Milk First fruit purée: apple (p40)*	*Breast or formula milk*	*Breast or formula milk*	*Breast or formula milk*
DAY 3	*Breast or formula milk*	*Breast or formula milk*	*Milk First vegetable purée: carrot (p36)*	*Breast or formula milk*	*Breast or formula milk*	*Breast or formula milk*
DAY 4	*Breast or formula milk*	*Breast or formula milk*	*Milk Cream of pear purée (p42)*	*Breast or formula milk*	*Breast or formula milk*	*Breast or formula milk*
DAY 5	*Breast or formula milk*	*Breast or formula milk*	*Milk First vegetable purée: potato or sweet potato (p36)*	*Breast or formula milk*	*Breast or formula milk*	*Breast or formula milk*
DAY 6	*Breast or formula milk*	*Breast or formula milk*	*Milk Apple and pear purée (p42)*	*Breast or formula milk*	*Breast or formula milk*	*Breast or formula milk*
DAY 7	*Breast or formula milk*	*Breast or formula milk*	*Milk Creamy vegetable purée (p39)*	*Breast or formula milk*	*Breast or formula milk*	*Breast or formula milk*

Sugar should not be added to weaning foods except when it is necessary to improve the palatability of sour fruit.

From weaning: weeks 3 and 4

	BREAKFAST	MID-MORNING	LUNCH	MID-AFTERNOON	SUPPER	BEDTIME
DAY 1	Mashed banana	Breast or formula milk	Mixed root vegetable purée (p36)	Breast or formula milk	Breast or formula milk	Breast or formula milk
DAY 2	First fruit purée: apple (p40)	Breast or formula milk	First vegetable purée: carrot (p36)	Breast or formula milk	Breast or formula milk	Breast or formula milk
DAY 3	Apple and pear purée (p42)	Breast or formula milk	Mixed root vegetable purée (p36)	Breast or formula milk	Breast or formula milk	Breast or formula milk
DAY 4	Cream of pear purée (p42)	Breast or formula milk	Sweet vegetable purée (p38)	Breast or formula milk	Breast or formula milk	Breast or formula milk
DAY 5	No-cook baby food: papaya (pawpaw) (p40)	Breast or formula milk	First vegetable purée: potato or sweet potato (p36)	Breast or formula milk	Breast or formula milk	Breast or formula milk
DAY 6	First fruit purée: pear (p40)	Breast or formula milk	Creamy vegetable purée (p39)	Breast or formula milk	Breast or formula milk	Breast or formula milk
DAY 7	Avocado and banana (p42)	Breast or formula milk	Baked sweet potato and carrot purée (p39)	Breast or formula milk	Breast or formula milk	Breast or formula milk

Sugar should not be added to weaning foods except when it is necessary to improve the palatability of sour fruit.

From weaning: after week 4

	BREAKFAST	MID-MORNING	LUNCH	MID-AFTERNOON	SUPPER	BEDTIME
DAY 1	*Peach, nectarine or plum and baby rice (p45)*	*Breast or formula milk*	*My first chicken purée (p59)*	*Breast or formula milk*	*Avocado and banana (p42)*	*Breast or formula milk*
DAY 2	*Apple, apricot and pear purée (p46)*	*Breast or formula milk*	*Potato and peas with a hint of mint (p45)*	*Breast or formula milk*	*Broccoli in cheese sauce (p75)*	*Breast or formula milk*
DAY 3	*No-cook baby food: banana (p40)*	*Breast or formula milk*	*Sweet potato and broccoli (p43)*	*Breast or formula milk*	*Butternut squash (pumpkin) and pear (p44)*	*Breast or formula milk*
DAY 4	*Blueberry and pear purée (p46)*	*Breast or formula milk*	*Braised beef with carrot, parsnip and sweet potato (p44)*	*Breast or formula milk*	*Mixed root vegetable purée (p36)*	*Breast or formula milk*
DAY 5	*Apple, apricot and pear purée (p46)*	*Breast or formula milk*	*No-cook baby food: e.g. avocado (p40)*	*Breast or formula milk*	*Sweet potato and broccoli (p43)*	*Breast or formula milk*
DAY 6	*Dried apricot with banana or baby rice and milk (p45)*	*Breast or formula milk*	*Parsnip and apple purée (p38)*	*Breast or formula milk*	*Sweet vegetable purée (p38)*	*Breast or formula milk*
DAY 7	*No-cook baby food: banana or papaya (pawpaw) (p40)*	*Breast or formula milk*	*Baked sweet potato and carrot purée (p39)*	*Breast or formula milk*	*Mixed root vegetable purée (p36)*	*Breast or formula milk*

Sugar should not be added to weaning foods except when it is necessary to improve the palatability of sour fruit.

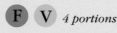

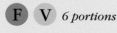
First vegetable purée From 6 months

In the first few weeks of weaning, make sure that carrots are cooked for quite a long time so that they are soft enough to purée to a smooth consistency. This method for cooking carrot also works with any of the other root vegetables, e.g. potatoes, sweet potatoes and swede. Cooking times will differ depending on which vegetable you choose.

350 g (12 oz) carrots

Peel and wash your chosen vegetable and chop or slice into even-sized pieces. Put in a steamer or colander set over boiling water and cook until tender (15 to 20 minutes). Alternatively, put the vegetables in a saucepan and pour over just enough boiling water to cover. Cover and simmer until soft (15 to 20 minutes).

Purée until very smooth together with some of the cooking liquid or some of the water in the bottom of the steamer. The amount of liquid you add really depends on your baby; you may need to add a little more if your baby finds it difficult to swallow.

To microwave, place the carrots in a suitable dish. Add 3 tablespoons of cooled boiled water and cover with microwave film. Pierce a few times and cook on high for 9 to 10 minutes, stirring halfway through cooking time. Blend to a purée adding some extra cooled boiled water to make a smooth consistency.

Spoon some of the purée into your baby's bowl and serve lukewarm.

Mixed root vegetable purée From 6 months

Mix and match a selection of three root vegetables. Use approximately 175 g (6 oz) of each but less of the parsnip as it has quite a strong taste. Choose from the vegetables below.

carrot / potato / sweet potato / pumpkin / swede / parsnip

Wash, peel and chop your chosen vegetables, place them in a saucepan and just cover with boiling water. Cook over a medium heat until tender (about 20 minutes). Blend the vegetables to a smooth purée using as much of the cooking liquid as necessary. Alternatively, steam the vegetables until tender, blending to a purée using some of the boiled water from the bottom of the steamer. You can also add some of your baby's usual milk as well as some of the cooking liquid. Spoon some of the purée into your baby's bowl and serve lukewarm.

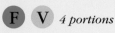

Butternut squash (pumpkin) *and* **pumpkin** *are easily digested and rarely cause allergies, therefore they make perfect weaning food.*

Healthy eating:

Don't use too much water when boiling vegetables and purée the vegetables with the cooking liquid as vitamins like vitamin C seep into the water.

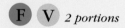

Parsnips *provide a good source of starch and fibre. They also contain the anti-oxidant vitamins C and E.*

Sweet vegetable purée From 6 months

Some of the more unusual vegetables like butternut squash are now more readily available in supermarkets and these can be made into delicious purées for your baby. The naturally sweet taste of butternut squash or pumpkin tends to be very popular with babies.

500 g (1 lb) butternut squash (pumpkin) or pumpkin

Peel and de-seed a squash or slice of pumpkin, then cut into small pieces. Place in a steamer and cook until tender (about 15 minutes). Alternatively, place in a pan with a little water, cover and simmer until tender. Drain and blend to a purée, adding a little of the cooking water if necessary.

Butternut squash can also be baked in the oven. Pre-heat an oven to 180°C/350°F/Gas Mark 4. Cut the squash in half, scoop out the seeds and brush with some melted unsalted butter. Cover with foil and bake in the oven until tender (about 1¼ hours).

To microwave, peel and dice the squash. Place in a suitable microwave dish and sprinkle over 3 tablespoons of water. Cover with microwave film, pierce and cook on high for 7 to 8 minutes, stirring halfway through. Let stand, covered, for 4 minutes. Purée and then spoon some of the purée into your baby's bowl and serve lukewarm.

Parsnip or carrot and apple purée From 6 months

Fruit and vegetable combinations work well together. Also try apple and carrot.

1 young parsnip or 2 medium carrots (approximately 125 g/4½ oz)
1 small apple

Scrub, top and tail the parsnip or carrots and cut into chunks. Place the chunks of parsnip or carrot in a steamer and cover and cook for 15 minutes. Peel, core and chop the apple, add to the parsnip or carrot and continue cooking for another 5 minutes. Drain and purée to a smooth consistency, adding a little of the water from the bottom of the steamer if necessary. Spoon some of the purée into your baby's bowl and serve lukewarm.

Baked sweet potato and carrot purée From 6 months

Baking sweet potato in the oven enhances its naturally sweet taste so this is a good purée to make if you are making a roast for the rest of the family, as you can just pop the sweet potato into the oven to cook alongside. It is also very tasty without the added carrot.

1 medium sweet potato (approximately 200 g/7 oz)
100 g (4 oz) carrots, peeled and sliced
2 to 3 tbsp your baby's usual milk

Pre-heat an oven to 190°C/375°F/Gas Mark 5. Wash and dry the sweet potato and prick all over with a fork. Bake in the oven until tender (about 45 minutes). Meanwhile, steam or boil the carrots until tender (about 20 minutes).

Alternatively, you can cook the sweet potato in a microwave. Pierce several holes in the potato with a fork. Place on at least two layers of absorbent kitchen paper. Microwave on high for 5 minutes, turning halfway through the cooking time. Let stand for 5 minutes. Peel and purée with a little of your baby's usual milk.

When the sweet potato is soft, allow to cool down a little, then cut it in half and scoop out the flesh. Purée together with the cooked carrot and the milk.

Creamy vegetable purée From 6 months

Stronger-tasting vegetables such as parsnip, carrot or broccoli can be given a more creamy mild taste by combining them with some baby rice and milk.

1 tbsp baby rice
3 tbsp your baby's usual milk
4 tbsp vegetable purée

Mix the baby rice and milk together according to the packet instructions, and stir into the vegetable purée until thoroughly combined.

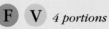 *4 portions*

Sweet potato *comes in two varieties: orange-fleshed and creamy-fleshed. Both have red skins and both are good sources of potassium, vitamin C and fibre. However, I prefer to use the orange-fleshed variety, which is also an excellent source of betacarotene. This helps to prevent certain types of cancer and mops up free radicals.*

SUPERFOODS

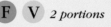 *2 portions*

Baby rice *should be the first cereal you introduce because it does not contain gluten, a protein found in wheat, oats, barley and rye that can cause food allergy if introduced before six months.*

SUPERFOODS

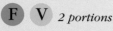

2 portions

SUPERFOODS

Apple *purée is very easy to digest, so makes great baby food. In America the BRAT diet (that is banana, rice, apples and toast) is popular with doctors for the relief of diarrhoea. Pectin, the soluble fibre in apples, also helps fight against constipation.*

V *1 to 2 portions*

SUPERFOODS

Papaya (pawpaw) *flesh is easy to swallow so it makes ideal weaning food. It is rich in vitamin C and betacarotene. 75 g (3 oz) of papaya will provide a young child's daily requirement of vitamin C. Papaya is also high in soluble fibre, which is important for normal bowel function. Papaya also contains enzymes, which aid digestion.*

First fruit purées From 6 months

Choose only sweet ripe fruit for your baby. Some apples like Cox's and Granny Smith can have quite a tart flavour and are not as sweet as other varieties.

2 medium dessert apples or 2 ripe pears, peeled and cored
2 tbsp water or pure unsweetened apple juice

Chop the apple or pear into small, even-sized pieces. Put the fruit into a heavy-based saucepan with the water, cover and cook over a low heat until tender (about 6 to 8 minutes for apples, 4 minutes for pears).

To microwave, chop the apple or pear into small, even-sized pieces. Place the fruit in a suitable dish, add 2 to 3 tablespoons of water and cover with microwave film. Pierce several times and then cook on full power until the fruit is tender (about 2 minutes).

Blend the fruit to a smooth purée using some of the cooking liquid. Spoon a little purée into your baby's bowl and serve lukewarm.

No-cook baby food From 6 months

Some mothers say that they just don't have the time to make their own baby food but there is nothing better for your baby than good quality fresh food. Here are some ideas for making delicious and nutritious baby food in minutes. So now there's no excuse! Always choose ripe fruit and serve straightaway.

Papaya (pawpaw)
Cut a small papaya in half, remove the black seeds and purée or mash the flesh of one half until smooth.

Avocado
Cut a small avocado in half, remove the stone, scoop out the flesh and mash together with a little of your baby's usual milk.

Banana
Peel the banana and mash with a fork. During the first stages of weaning add a little milk if necessary to thin down the consistency and add a familiar taste.

4 portions

SUPERFOODS

Pears *are one of the least allergenic foods so they make great weaning food.*

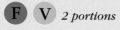

 1 portion

SUPERFOODS

Bananas *are full of slow-release sugars, which provide sustained energy. They make perfect portable baby food as they come in their own easy-to-peel packaging. They are also good for the treatment of diarrhoea and constipation.*

F V *2 portions*

SUPERFOODS

Baby rice *is gluten-free, easily digested and has a milky taste that helps to ease your baby's transition from a purely milky diet to solids. It is a good thickener for runny purées like pear, peach or plum.*

Apple and pear purée From 6 months

Apple and pear blend well together. You could add a small cinnamon stick to introduce a new flavour. Simply remove the stick before puréeing the fruit or add a pinch of ground cinnamon when cooking. Choose sweet apples like Pink Lady or Royal Gala.

2 dessert apples, peeled, cored and chopped
2 ripe pears, peeled and cored and chopped
4 tbsp pure unsweetened apple juice or water
2 tbsp water

Put the fruit into a heavy-based saucepan with the apple juice and water, cover and cook over a low heat until tender (6 to 8 minutes). Blend the fruit to a smooth purée. Spoon a little purée into your baby's bowl and serve lukewarm.

Avocado and banana From 6 months

¼ avocado
½ small ripe banana
1 to 2 tbsp your baby's usual milk

Mash the avocado together with the banana and the milk. You can substitute the flesh of half a small papaya (pawpaw) for the banana in this recipe. If using papaya, the milk is then optional.

Cream of pear purée From 6 months

2 small ripe pears, peeled, cored and cut into chunks
1 tbsp baby rice
1 tbsp your baby's usual milk

Put the pear into a small saucepan and cover and cook for 2 to 3 minutes. Blend to a smooth purée. Mix together the baby rice and milk and stir this into the pear purée.

Vegetables at 6 months after first tastes accepted

Naturally sweet-tasting root vegetable purées are easy to digest and are ideal for early weaning. But after a few weeks you can introduce stronger-tasting vegetables like broccoli.

Courgette (zucchini)

Courgette is best mixed with another vegetable and it goes well with sweet potatoes, carrots, pumpkins, potatoes and swede. Wash, trim and slice 250 g (8 oz) courgettes. Place in a steamer and cook until tender (10 to 12 minutes). Alternatively, place in a pan with a little boiling water. Cover and simmer gently until tender (6 to 8 minutes).

To microwave, place the slices of courgette in a microwaveable dish, add 1 tablespoon of water. Cover with microwave film, pierce the film and microwave on high until tender (about 6 minutes). Stir halfway through. Let stand for 3 minutes before turning into a purée.

Cauliflower or broccoli

Place 250 g (8 oz) small cauliflower or broccoli florets in a steamer and cook until tender (about 10 minutes). Drain and blend to a purée with a little of the boiled water from the steamer. Alternatively, add just enough boiling water to cover the vegetables, then cover and simmer until tender (about 10 minutes).

To microwave, place the florets in a microwaveable dish, sprinkle over 2 tablespoons of water and cover with microwave film. Pierce the film and microwave on high until tender (about 6 minutes), stirring halfway through. Let stand for 4 minutes then purée with a little of your baby's usual milk or boiled water to make a smooth purée. Broccoli has quite a strong taste and is best mixed with potato, sweet potato, pumpkin or swede or a cheese sauce (see p.75).

Sweet potato and broccoli From 6 months

200 g (7 oz) sweet potatoes, peeled and diced
60 g (2½ oz) broccoli florets

Steam the sweet potato and broccoli until tender (sweet potato: about 12 minutes; broccoli: 7 to 8 minutes). Purée together with a little of the water from the bottom of the steamer. Spoon some of the purée into your baby's bowl and serve lukewarm.

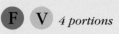 *4 portions*

Courgettes (zucchini) *are a good source of betacarotene but most of the nutrients lie in the skin, so do not peel them.*

Broccoli *is a true SuperFood as it is a great source of vitamin C and also contains betacarotene, folic acid, iron, potassium and anti-cancer phytonutrients.*

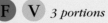 *3 portions*

Broccoli *is best steamed or microwaved as boiling it in water halves its vitamin C content. If your baby isn't keen on the taste, mix it with a sweet-tasting vegetable like sweet potato, swede or butternut squash (pumpkin).*

SUPERFOODS

SUPERFOODS

F *5 portions*

SUPERFOODS

Red meat *provides the best source of iron for your baby. It is important to introduce iron-rich foods as a baby's iron reserves inherited from his mother start to run out at 6 months. Breast milk does not contain adequate levels of iron.*

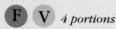

F **V** *4 portions*

SUPERFOODS

Butternut squash (pumpkin) *provides an excellent source of betacarotene.*

Braised beef with carrot, parsnip and sweet potato From 6 months

This recipe makes a good introduction to red meat. The root vegetables give the meat a smooth texture and a flavour that babies like. You can also introduce chicken to your baby once first tastes are accepted.

1 small red onion (approx. 75 g/3 oz), chopped

1 clove garlic, crushed

1 tbsp olive oil

150 g (4½ oz) lean braising steak, cut into pieces

2 tbsp flour

150 g (4½ oz) carrots, peeled and sliced

75 g (3 oz) parsnip, peeled and sliced

225 g (8 oz) sweet potato, peeled and chopped

1 bay leaf

1 tbsp chopped parsley

375 ml (12 fl oz) unsalted chicken stock

Heat the vegetable oil in a heavy bottomed saucepan or small casserole. Sauté the onion and garlic for 3 to 4 minutes until softened. Toss the pieces of steak in flour and sauté until sealed. Add the carrots, parsnip, sweet potato, bay leaf and parsley to the pan and pour over the stock. Bring to the boil and then simmer for about 1 hour 45 minutes or until the meat is tender. Blend, adding as much of the cooking liquid as necessary.

Butternut squash (pumpkin) and pear From 6 months

The naturally sweet taste of butternut squash is generally very popular with babies and it combines very well with a variety of fruits. Try also butternut squash and peach when fresh ripe, juicy peaches are in season.

1 butternut squash (pumpkin) (about 350 g/12 oz), peeled, de-seeded and chopped

1 ripe juicy pear, peeled, cored and chopped

Steam the butternut squash until tender (about 12 minutes). Add the chopped pear and continue to steam for about 3 minutes. Purée with about 2 tablespoons of the water from the bottom of the steamer. You can also cut the butternut squash in half, brush with melted butter, cover loosely with foil and bake in the oven at 180°C/350°F/Gas Mark 4 until tender.

Potato and peas with a hint of mint

From 6 months

F V *2 portions*

1 large potato (approx. 200 g/7 oz), peeled and diced	75 g (3 oz) frozen peas
	2 sprigs of mint

Put the diced potato into a saucepan and pour over boiling water. Cover and cook for 6 minutes. Add the frozen peas and mint and cover and simmer for 5 minutes. Remove the sprigs of mint and purée the vegetables in a mouli to get rid of the indigestible husks of the peas. Spoon some of the purée into your baby's bowl and serve lukewarm. You could also make this recipe with sweet potato and peas.

Fruits at 6 months after first tastes accepted

Naturally fruits can be puréed on their own or mixed with a little baby rice, banana or pear. Make sure that you choose fruit that is sweet and ripe.

Peaches and nectarines

Score a cross on the base of the fruit, then submerge in boiling water for 1 minute. Drain, skin and chop the peach or nectarine, discarding the stone, and then purée.

Plums and apricots

Choose sweet ripe plums or apricots. Skin by submerging the fruit in boiling water (see above) and cut into quarters and discard the stones. Steam for a few minutes until soft and then purée. Both plums and apricots combine well with puréed apple.

Melons

Take a small wedge of melon, scoop out the seeds and discard. Peel away the skin and cut the flesh into chunks. Purée until smooth. Melon is also good with mashed banana or avocado.

Dried apricots and peaches

Simmer ready-to-eat dried apricots in water until soft, then purée in a mouli to get rid of the tough skins and add a little of the cooking liquid to make a smooth purée. Dried apricot purée is good mixed with baby rice and milk, mashed banana, apple or pear purée.

SUPERFOODS

Mint *aids digestion, which is one of the reasons why some people like to drink mint tea.*

F V

SUPERFOODS

Peaches *provide a good source of vitamin C and the soft flesh is easy to digest.*

Apricots *are a good source of betacarotene and also contain fibre.*

Cantaloupe (rock) melon *is the most nutritious variety of melon. It is very sweet and rich in vitamin C and betacarotene.*

Dried apricots *are a great source of betacarotene and are a good source of iron and potassium. The drying process increases their concentration.*

1 to 2 portions

Blueberries *are rich in vitamin C and also contain betacarotene. The blue pigment anthocyanin in the skin of the blueberries helps protect us against cancer. Blueberries have the highest antioxidant capacity of all fruits, mainly because of the anthocyanins in their skin.*

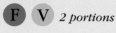 *2 portions*

Dried apricots *are one of nature's great health foods. It is best to choose semi-dried apricots as they are nice and soft, but make sure they have not been treated with sulphur dioxide (E220) before drying in order to preserve the bright orange colour and to prevent fungal growth. This substance can trigger an asthma attack in susceptible babies. Dried fruits are rich in potassium which helps counteract the high salt content of fast foods like burgers and chips. Dried apricots make a good high-energy snack.*

Blueberry and pear purée From 6 months

This is a quick and easy purée to make and the blueberries turn it a wonderful deep purple. Berry fruits can sometimes cause reactions in allergic young babies so don't give them to your baby if there is any sign of a reaction and consult your doctor for advice.

1 large ripe juicy pear, peeled, cored and chopped
50 g (2 oz) blueberries
½ tbsp baby rice

Put the fruit into a saucepan and simmer for about 5 minutes. Purée and stir in the baby rice. Spoon some of the purée into your baby's bowl and serve lukewarm.

Apple, apricot and pear purée From 6 months

This makes a delicious and nutritious combination of fruits. It can be mixed either with baby rice, as in the recipe below, or it is good with mashed banana. Banana, however, cannot be frozen so freeze the purée in individual containers without the baby rice and add the mashed banana just before serving, once you have defrosted and re-heated your baby's meal.

1 apple, peeled, cored and chopped
60 g (2½ oz) dried apricots, roughly chopped
4 tbsp water
1 ripe pear, peeled, cored and chopped
1 tbsp baby rice
2 tbsp your baby's usual milk

Place the apple and dried apricots in a saucepan with the water. Cover and simmer for 5 minutes. Add the pear and continue to simmer for 2 minutes. Purée the fruit until smooth. In a small bowl, mix the baby rice with the milk until smooth and stir into the fruit purée.

7 to 9 months:
exploring new tastes and textures

Babies develop rapidly between seven and nine months and your baby will soon be sitting in a high chair. She will be ready for stronger tastes and more challenging textures.

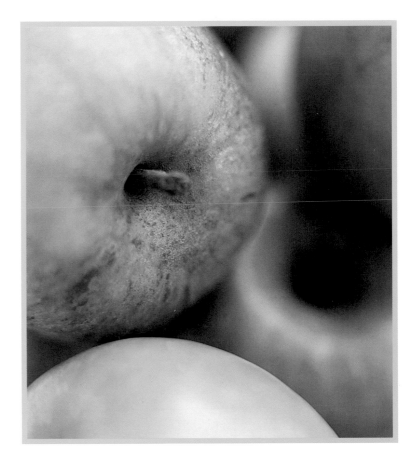

The next hurdles

By the age of seven months, your baby should be eating three meals a day. The quantity will vary from child to child but by this stage your baby is ready to enjoy a wide variety of tastes. This is a stage of quite rapid development and your baby will spend many more hours awake. Whereas a six-month-old baby still needs to be supported when you are feeding him, a nine-month-old is usually strong enough to sit in a high chair.

Try to make eating a sociable event and let your baby join you at mealtimes whenever possible. Never force a baby to eat something he doesn't want. Instead, let your baby's appetite be your guide. As long as your baby is happy and continues to grow, he should be fine.

Babies should have 500 to 600 ml (18 to 20 fl oz) of formula or breast milk each day up to the age of one year. A portion of the milk intake can come from dairy products like cheese and yoghurt. If your baby is not hungry at mealtimes, you may find that cutting down on the amount of milk your baby drinks will mean that he is hungrier for his solids and therefore not so fussy about the texture of his food.

Introducing more texture

Having introduced a wide range of single ingredient purées, you can now combine foods to make tasty meals for your baby. As teeth begin to emerge (see overleaf), introduce slightly coarser textures into your baby's food and soft finger foods. Your baby will probably still mostly use his gums to chew and it is surprising how efficient these are at chomping their way through food. It is not a good idea to continue giving only smooth purées for too long or your baby may become lazy about chewing and have difficulty developing the tongue movement needed to cope with solids.

New foods to introduce

At this age, babies should eat foods each day from each of the food groups: starches, fruit and vegetables, protein, milk and dairy products (see pages 13 to 16).

* *Wheat-based foods such as pasta or bread.*
* *Low sugar cereals like porridge, Weetabix and Ready Brek. Avoid large amounts of high-fibre foods like bran as these are difficult for babies to digest and can deplete the body of vital nutrients.*
* *Dairy products, e.g. cheese or yoghurt made with whole milk. Low-fat dairy products such as low-fat yoghurt are not suitable as they are too low in calories for growing babies. Avoid soft cheeses like camembert or brie because of the risk of listeriosis.*
* *Cow's milk is low in iron and vitamin D so babies should continue with breast or formula milk for the first year.*

However, cow's milk can be used in cooking or with your baby's cereal.

* *Lean red meat and poultry.*
* *Mild-tasting fish such as plaice (flounder), cod and salmon. Many children grow up disliking fish, which is a great shame, so I try very hard to come up with really tasty fish recipes.*
* *Stronger-flavoured vegetables such as leeks, spinach, onions and mushrooms. At eight or nine months try steamed vegetables like carrot sticks or broccoli florets.*
* *Citrus fruits.*
* *Berry fruits (sieve to get rid of the seeds).*
* *Stronger-tasting fruits such as mango.*
* *Pulses, e.g. lentils, split peas.*
* *Tofu.*
* *Eggs: hard-boiled or well cooked such as in an omelette.*

For a gradual introduction you could mix some mashed or grated food with some of your baby's favourite purées. Don't expect him to be thrilled by this change as lumps take a bit of getting used to. Some babies will cope very well with chopped food at nine months but others still prefer smoother textures.

Another way to introduce texture into your baby's meals is to prepare a fairly smooth purée and then add some tiny cooked pasta shapes. For older children you can mix cooked pasta shapes with bite-sized pieces of cooked vegetables like carrots, french beans and broccoli. Chewing and swallowing lumpy food is linked to speech development. Some babies prefer finger foods that melt in the mouth, like banana, peach or fingers of toast, to lumpy food.

Learning to eat red meat

I think that sometimes we mistakenly believe that babies don't like the taste of certain foods when, in fact, it is the texture that they object to. This is often the case with meat. Unless you choose to bring up your child as a vegetarian, red meat is an excellent food as it provides the best source of iron, which is vitally important for both physical and mental development. Babies are born with a store of iron that lasts for about six months. After this it is important to make sure they get the iron they need from their food. A baby's iron requirements are particularly high between six and twelve months.

The trouble is that meat can be very chewy and so I have found that the best way to make it more palatable is to combine it with root vegetables or pasta, both of which will help to produce a much smoother and easier to swallow texture. I find that when cooking minced meat for older babies, for example as a Bolognese sauce, it is still much better received if once the meat is cooked it is then chopped for a few seconds in a food processor.

Self-feeding

Let your baby experiment with feeding herself, using her fingers or a spoon. The more independent your growing baby, the sooner she will master the art of feeding herself. See page 70 for suitable finger foods.

Equipment

High chair: Once your baby can support her head and upper body, she can use a high chair. But if your baby is active, don't put her there until her meal is ready in case she gets upset at being confined to one place for too long. Put her in a safety harness so that she can't wriggle and fall out. Meals are not just about nutrition, they are a time for being sociable, so let her join in with family meals by pulling the high chair up to the table.

Bowls and spoons: A plastic bowl with a suction pad on the base is a good idea at this age; throwing food on the floor is often as much fun as eating it. As soon as you think she is ready, give her a plastic spoon and fork: she can experiment with feeding herself. Getting food onto a spoon is easier if the food is in a bowl rather than on a plate.

Feeding cups: Many babies can learn to drink from a feeder cup around the age of six months. Start with a double-handled cup with a soft spout and snap-tight lid. There are many varieties including no-spill cups and cups with a one-way valve control so that even if the cup is turned upside down, no liquid will come out. Eventually graduate to an open cup.

Your baby's first teeth

Your baby will be teething from around six to eighteen months and so gums may be sore and your child may be quite unsettled and not interested in food. A chilled teething ring can help soothe sore gums. You could also give chilled raw vegetables like sticks of carrot or cucumber. Rubbing an infant teething gel on to the gums may help – they contain local anaesthetics and can be prescribed by a GP, who is the best person to discuss whether they are suitable or not.

Teeth begin to erupt from six months onwards and four to eight teeth are usually present by the age of twelve months. You should start brushing your baby's teeth as soon as the first one appears. Brush your child's teeth thoroughly twice a day, using a small, pea-sized blob of children's toothpaste on a small baby toothbrush with soft fibres. Do not put a lot of toothpaste on your child's toothbrush, particularly in areas where fluoride is already added to tap water. Too much fluoride can cause dental fluorosis, which can permanently discolour children's teeth. Alternatively, you could wrap a clean flannel around your finger and gently rub the teeth and gums. Brush teeth twice a day.

Ways to prevent caries
• *Use a cup as soon as your child is able to use one.*
• *Diluted juice with meals is fine but it is best to give water or milk between meals.*
• *Do not put your child to bed with a bottle.*
• *Do not use bottles to feed juice or as comforters.*
• *Do not bottle feed after one year of age.*

Baby bottle tooth decay

Drinking from a bottle is worse for teeth than drinking from a cup because the juice is in contact with the teeth for longer. Nursing bottle caries, also known as baby bottle tooth decay, occurs when a young baby or small child is frequently given sugary drinks in a bottle. The bacteria present on teeth uses sugar to produce acid, which attacks tooth enamel, which leads to tooth decay. It is even worse to give a baby a bottle to suck at night when there is less saliva than usual, which results in sugar clinging to the teeth. It is much better to give water between meals, reserving fruit juice for mealtimes only. If your child insists on a bottle to take to bed then use water. It is a good idea to start using a lidded cup with a spout from the age of six or seven months and eventually move on to a cup. Try to dispense with bottles by the time your baby is one year old (see also page 68).

Tooth-friendly snacks
• **Vegetable sticks on their own or with a dip.**
• **Cheese or cheese on toast.**
• **Sugar-free teething biscuits or rusks.**
• **Fingers of toast or bagels.**
• **Cream cheese with mini-bread sticks, rice cakes or oatcakes.**
• **Mini-sandwiches with peanut butter, Marmite or Promite, egg mayonnaise (make sure it is pasteurised).**
• **A bowl of home-made soup or fresh soup from a carton.**
• **Mini-salads, e.g. mozzarella and tomato, pasta, tuna and sweetcorn.**
• **Fresh fruit. Biting on frozen fruit can help numb the pain.**

Healthy eating: *Teething often causes your baby to dribble, so it is a good idea to put a little petroleum jelly around your baby's mouth and chin to help prevent them from becoming dry and red.*

Meal planner

Vary the desserts with lunch and supper. Give your baby some fresh fruit like a banana or grated apple, fruit purée and occasionally other desserts like ice cream, rice pudding, yoghurt and fromage frais.

	BREAKFAST	MID-MORNING	LUNCH	MID-AFTERNOON	SUPPER	BEDTIME
DAY 1	Breast or formula milk My favourite porridge (p65) Fruit	Breast or formula milk	Chicken, sweet potato and pea purée (p57)	Breast or formula milk	Vegetable purée with tomato and cheese (p62)	Breast or formula milk
DAY 2	Breast or formula milk Cereal Banana	Breast or formula milk	My first fish purée (p61)	Breast or formula milk	Eat your greens purée (p57)	Breast or formula milk
DAY 3	Breast or formula milk Apricot, papaya (pawpaw) and tofu with baby rice and milk (p64)	Breast or formula milk	My first chicken purée (p59)	Breast or formula milk	Carrot purée with lentils and cheese (p55)	Breast or formula milk
DAY 4	Breast or formula milk Cheese on toast Strawberry, peach and apple purée (p64)	Breast or formula milk	Old-fashioned beef casserole (p60)	Breast or formula milk	Potato, leek, carrot and pea purée (p61)	Breast or formula milk
DAY 5	Breast or formula milk Cereal and yoghurt	Breast or formula milk	Fruity chicken with butternut squash (pumpkin) (p59)	Breast or formula milk	Tasty trio of root vegetables (p54)	Breast or formula milk
DAY 6	Breast or formula milk Well-cooked scrambled egg with fingers of toast (p64)	Breast or formula milk	Cherub's chowder (p62)	Breast or formula milk	Vegetable purée with tomato and cheese (p62) Fingers of toast	Breast or formula milk
DAY 7	Breast or formula milk Apple, pear and prune with oats (p65) Raisin toast fingers	Breast or formula milk	Chicken, sweet potato and pea purée (p57)	Breast or formula milk	Chicken liver with vegetables and apple (p60)	Breast or formula milk

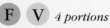

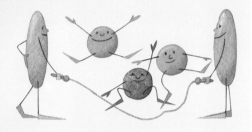

Lentils *are a good source of protein and fibre. They are also a rich source of potassium, zinc and folic acid. Both cheese and lentils are good nutrient-dense foods for growing babies.*

F V *6 portions*

Sweet potatoes *are rich in vitamins C and E and betacarotene so sometimes it's a good idea to substitute them for ordinary potatoes.*

Healthy eating:
Frozen vegetables for baby purées can be just as nutritious as fresh.

Carrot purée with lentils and cheese

50 g (2 oz) peeled and finely chopped onion
¹/₂ tbsp vegetable oil
25 g (1 oz) red lentils
200 g (7 oz) carrots, peeled and sliced
15 g (¹/₂ oz) unsalted butter
2 tomatoes, skinned, de-seeded and roughly chopped
50 g (2 oz) Cheddar cheese, grated

In a saucepan, sauté the onion in the vegetable oil until softened (3 to 4 minutes). Rinse the lentils and drain and add to the onion. Add the carrots and pour over 400 ml (13 fl oz) boiling water. Bring to the boil, then cover the saucepan and cook over a medium heat for 25 minutes. Melt the butter in a saucepan and sauté the tomatoes until mushy, then stir in the Cheddar cheese.

Drain the carrot and lentil mixture and reserve the cooking liquid. Combine the carrots and lentils together with 125 ml (4 fl oz) of the cooking liquid and the tomato and cheese mixture in a food processor and purée to a smooth consistency.

Tasty trio of root vegetables

The orange-fleshed sweet potato is richer in nutrients than the white-fleshed sweet potato. You can buy unsalted vegetable stock cubes from a supermarket.

25 g (1 oz) unsalted butter
60 g (2¹/₂ oz) washed and sliced leeks
300 g (10 oz) sweet potatoes, peeled and diced
75 g (3 oz) carrots, peeled and sliced
50 g (2 oz) parsnips, peeled and diced
375 ml (12 fl oz) vegetable stock

Melt the butter in a saucepan and sauté the leek for 3 to 4 minutes. Add the sweet potatoes, carrots and parsnips, pour over the stock, bring to the boil and then cover and simmer for 20 minutes. Purée in a food processor or mash for older babies.

Chicken, sweet potato and pea purée

 6 portions

Not only does this taste delicious, it is also packed full of vitamins since both sweet potatoes and carrots are excellent sources of vitamin A. The naturally sweet taste and smooth texture of sweet potato makes this an ideal purée for introducing young babies to their first taste of chicken.

½ small onion, peeled and chopped

1 tbsp vegetable oil

100 g (4 oz) chicken breast, cut into pieces

350 g (12 oz) sweet potatoes, peeled and diced

1 medium carrot, peeled and sliced

300 ml (10 fl oz) unsalted chicken
  stock

75 g (3 oz) frozen peas

Heat the vegetable oil in a saucepan and sauté the onion for 2 to 3 minutes. Add the chicken and sauté until sealed. Add the sweet potatoes and carrots and pour over the chicken stock. Bring to the boil, then cover and simmer for 20 minutes. Add the frozen peas and continue to cook for a further 5 minutes. Purée in a food processor.

Eat your greens purée

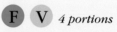 *4 portions*

It's a good idea to introduce your baby to the flavour of green vegetables early on. However, sometimes they find the taste of some vegetables too strong so it can be a good idea to mix stronger-tasting vegetables like broccoli together with potato. You could also make this purée using other green vegetables like spinach or courgette (zucchini).

40 g (1½ oz) peeled and chopped onion

15 g (½ oz) unsalted butter

250 g (9 oz) potatoes, peeled and diced

375 ml (12 fl oz) unsalted vegetable stock
  or water

50 g (2 oz) broccoli florets

50 g (2 oz) frozen peas

Sauté the onion in the butter until softened but not coloured (about 5 minutes). Add the potato, pour over the stock or water, cover and bring to the boil and then cook for 10 minutes. Add the broccoli florets and cook for 3 minutes. Then add the peas and cook for a further 3 minutes. Purée in a mouli.

SUPERFOODS

SUPERFOODS

My first chicken purée

Chicken blends well with many vegetables and mixing it with root vegetables helps to give this purée a smooth texture to make a good introduction to chicken.

50 g (2 oz) washed and sliced leeks
1 tbsp vegetable oil
75 g (3 oz) chicken breast, cut into chunks
200 g (7 oz) potatoes, peeled and diced
175 g (6 oz) carrots, peeled and sliced

2 plum tomatoes, skinned, de-seeded
  and chopped
250 ml (8 fl oz) unsalted chicken stock

Sauté the leeks in the vegetable oil until softened (about 3 minutes). Then add the chicken and sauté until it has sealed. Add the potatoes, carrots and tomatoes and pour over the chicken stock. Bring to the boil, then reduce the heat and cover and simmer for 20 minutes. Purée in a food processor.

Fruity chicken with butternut squash (pumpkin)

1 tbsp vegetable oil
60 g (2½ oz) peeled and chopped onion
120g (4½ oz) chicken breast, cut into chunks
300 g (10 oz) butternut squash (pumpkin), peeled, de-seeded and chopped
300 ml (10 fl oz) unsalted chicken stock
1 small apple, peeled, cored and chopped

Heat the oil in a saucepan and sauté the onion until softened. Add the chicken breast and sauté for 3 to 4 minutes. Add the butternut squash, pour over the stock, cover and bring to the boil and simmer for about 10 minutes. Add the apple and cook until the chicken is cooked through and the butternut squash is tender (about 10 minutes). Purée in a food processor to the desired consistency.

 F *5 portions*

Chicken *is a growth food as it is packed with protein and vitamin B12, which is not found in plant foods. Chicken also naturally contains fat, which is used for energy and growth. It is very important that children aged six to nine months start to regularly eat foods containing adequate amounts of protein.*

SUPERFOODS

 F *6 portions*

Butternut squash (pumpkin) *is very appealing to babies as they love its sweet taste – and it is a very good source of the antioxidant betacarotene.*

SUPERFOODS

SUPERFOODS

Chicken liver *provides a good source of vitamins and iron. Babies are born with a store of iron that lasts for about six months so after this time it is important to ensure they get the iron that they need from their solids.*

Chicken liver with vegetables and apple

100 g (4 oz) chicken liver

25 g (1 oz) peeled and chopped onion

1 tbsp vegetable oil

1 medium carrot, peeled and sliced

1 large potato, peeled and diced

½ small apple, peeled, cored and chopped

250 ml (8 fl oz) unsalted chicken stock

Clean the livers, removing any fat or gristle, and slice them. Sauté the onion in the vegetable oil until softened. Add the sliced liver and sauté until it has changed colour (about 1 minute). Add the carrots, potatoes and apples, pour over the stock and simmer for 20 minutes. Purée in a food processor.

SUPERFOODS

Red meat *provides the best and most easily absorbed source of iron. A baby's iron requirements are particularly high between six and twelve months.*

Healthy eating:

Never show your own dislike of food to your child – personally I am not madly keen on liver but my three children loved it as babies!

Old-fashioned beef casserole

The onions and carrots in this recipe give the beef a wonderful flavour and the long slow cooking makes it lovely and tender.

1 onion, peeled and sliced

1½ tbsp vegetable oil

225 g (8 oz) lean stewing (blade or round) steak, cut into chunks

2 carrots, peeled and sliced

300 g (10 oz) potatoes, peeled and diced

1 tbsp parsley

450 ml (16 fl oz) unsalted chicken or beef stock

Pre-heat an oven to 150°C/300°F/Gas Mark 2. Sauté the onion in the vegetable oil in a flame-proof casserole until lightly golden. Add the beef and sauté until browned. Add the carrots, potatoes and parsley, pour over the stock and bring the mixture to the boil.

Cover with a lid and transfer the casserole to the pre-heated oven and cook until the meat is really tender (about 2 hours). Add extra stock if necessary. Blend to a purée of the desired consistency or, for older babies, chop into small pieces.

My first fish purée

 4 portions

150 g (4½ oz) plaice (flounder) fillets,
  skinned

peppercorns

1 bay leaf

sprig of parsley

150 ml (5 fl oz) milk

150 g (5 oz) carrots, peeled and sliced

25 g (1 oz) frozen peas

15 g (½ oz) unsalted butter

1 tbsp flour

25 g (1 oz) Cheddar cheese, grated

Put the fillets of fish into a saucepan together with the peppercorns, bay leaf and parsley and pour over the milk. Simmer until the fish is cooked (about 5 minutes). Strain and reserve the cooking liquid but discard the peppercorns, bay leaf and parsley.

Put the carrots into a saucepan and pour over 300 ml (10 fl oz) boiling water. Cover and cook over a medium heat for 15 minutes, add the peas and cook for a further 5 minutes. Drain, reserving the water.

To make the cheese sauce, melt the butter in a saucepan and stir in the flour to make a roux, then gradually whisk in the reserved cooking liquid from the fish. Bring to the boil and then simmer until thickened (1 to 2 minutes). Remove from the heat and stir in the grated cheese. Mix in the drained vegetables and the flaked fish, checking to make sure there are no bones. Blend to a smooth purée for young babies and, if necessary, you can add a little more milk or some of the cooking water from the carrots and peas to thin it out.

Fish is an excellent low-fat source of protein and it is important to encourage a liking for fish early on. I find that one of the best fish to introduce to young babies is plaice (flounder) as it purées to a smooth consistency. Here I have mixed it with a creamy cheese sauce and vegetables so this recipe provides an excellent source of protein, calcium and vitamins.

SUPERFOODS

Potato, leek, carrot and pea purée

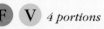 *4 portions*

25 g (1 oz) unsalted butter

60 g (2½ oz) washed and sliced leeks

175 g (6 oz) potatoes, peeled and diced

1 medium carrot, peeled and sliced

300 ml (10 fl oz) unsalted chicken stock or vegetable stock

50 g (2 oz) frozen peas

Melt the butter in a saucepan and sauté the leek for 3 to 4 minutes. Add the potatoes and carrots and pour over the chicken stock. Bring to the boil, then reduce the heat, cover and cook for 15 minutes. Add the frozen peas and continue to cook until the vegetables are tender (3–4 minutes). Purée in a food processor or with a hand-held blender.

Potatoes contain vitamin C, and are a good source of potassium. They also blend well with most vegetables.

SUPERFOODS

Healthy eating:

Peel potatoes just before cooking. Don't soak in water as they will then lose their vitamin C.

F *3 portions*

SUPERFOODS

Fish *should be cooked on the day it is bought to retain its freshness. Cod is high in protein and vitamin B12.*

V *6 portions*

SUPERFOODS

Cauliflower *provides a good source of vitamin C and also contains folic acid and glucosinolates, which are sulphurous compounds that help to protect against certain forms of cancer.*

Did you know?

Glucosinolates were once thought to be toxic and are even natural pesticides. They are now known to have anti-cancer properties.

Cherub's chowder

This recipe also makes a good introduction to fish for small babies.

50 g (2 oz) peeled and chopped onion
1 tbsp vegetable oil
175 g (6 oz) potatoes, peeled and diced
50 g (2 oz) carrots, peeled and sliced
375 ml (12 fl oz) unsalted chicken,
    vegetable or fish stock

150 g (5 oz) skinned cod fillet
25 g (1 oz) frozen peas
25 g (1 oz) frozen sweetcorn

Sauté the onion in the vegetable oil until softened but not coloured. Add the potatoes and carrots, pour over the stock and cover and simmer for 15 minutes. Cut the fish into chunks and add the vegetables together with the frozen peas and sweetcorn and cook for 5 minutes. Purée with as much of the cooking liquid as necessary to make the desired consistency. For older babies, simply mash with a fork, adding as much liquid as you like.

Vegetable purée with tomato and cheese

Mixing vegetables together with some grated Cheddar cheese and fresh tomatoes gives them a lovely flavour. This purée will provide your baby with both vitamin C and betacarotene.

2 large carrots (approx. 200 g/8 oz), peeled and sliced
100 g (4 oz) cauliflower, cut into small florets
a generous knob of unsalted butter
3 tomatoes, skinned, de-seeded and roughly chopped
75 g (3 oz) Cheddar cheese, grated

Put the carrots and cauliflower into a saucepan and just cover with boiling water. Cover and cook for 20 minutes. Meanwhile, melt the knob of butter and sauté the tomatoes for about 2 minutes until slightly mushy, then stir in the grated cheese until melted. Blend the vegetables together with the cheese and tomato sauce.

SUPERFOODS

Bananas and cherries *contain high levels of potassium, which works with sodium to maintain the body's water balance, regulate blood pressure and maintain a normal heartbeat.*

SUPERFOODS

Tofu *is soya bean curd made from soya milk. It is a perfect vegetarian source of protein and rich in many nutrients including iron, potassium and calcium. It is a good source of calcium and eating tofu may help to prevent certain forms of heart disease and cancer.*

SUPERFOODS

Strawberries *contain more vitamin C than other berry fruits. 100g will give an adult almost twice the daily recommended amount. They are also a good source of fibre and betacarotene and can help protect the body against cancer.*

Cherry and banana purée

6 sweet ripe cherries
1 very small banana
1 tsp baby rice (optional)

Wash the cherries, remove the stalks and put them into a small saucepan. Just cover with boiling water, then cover and simmer for about 4 minutes. Allow the cherries to cool down a little, remove the stones and press through a sieve to get rid of the skins. Mash the banana and mix with the sieved cherries. If you like, stir in the baby rice.

Apricot, papaya (pawpaw) and tofu

Although tofu has almost no taste of its own, it combines well with either fruit or vegetables to make a creamy purée. There are two types of tofu – soft or firm tofu.

100 g (4 oz) dried apricots
1 large papaya (pawpaw) (550 g/1 lb 3 oz), de-seeded, peeled and chopped
100 g (4 oz) soft tofu

Put the apricots in a small saucepan and pour over 250 ml (8 fl oz) boiling water. Cover and cook until tender (about 5 minutes). Drain the apricots and purée together with the papaya and tofu until smooth.

Strawberry peach and apple purée

This is delicious on its own or mixed with a little baby rice or mashed bananas.

4 strawberries (approx. 75 g/3 oz)
1 large, juicy, ripe peach, peeled, stoned and cut into pieces
1 apple, peeled, cored and cut into pieces

Put the fruit in a small, heavy-based saucepan, cover and simmer for 4 to 5 minutes. Blend to a purée.

Apple, pear and prune with oats

You could also make this recipe with soft ready-to-eat dried figs instead of prunes.

2 tbsp porridge oats
4 tbsp pure unsweetened apple juice
2 tbsp water
1 small apple, peeled, cored and chopped
2 stoned prunes, chopped
1 small ripe pear, peeled, cored and chopped

Put the oats, apple juice and water in a saucepan, bring to the boil and simmer for 2 minutes. Add the chopped apple, prunes and pear and cover and simmer for 3 minutes, stirring occasionally. Purée to the desired consistency.

My favourite porridge

This was my children's favourite breakfast when they were babies. Not only does it taste great, it is also packed full of nutritious ingredients. Dried apricots are a good source of betacarotene, iron and also contain fibre.

150 ml (5 fl oz) milk
15 g (¹/₂ oz) porridge oats
6 ready-to-eat dried apricots (3 tablespoons, chopped)
1 large ripe pear, peeled, cored and cut into pieces

Put the milk, porridge oats and chopped apricots in a small saucepan, bring to the boil and then simmer, stirring occasionally, for 3 minutes. Purée together with the chopped pear in a hand blender.

F **V** *2 portions*

Prunes *are a good source of instant energy, fibre and iron. They help with constipation as they are a natural laxative.*

SUPERFOODS

Healthy eating:
For older children, tinned prunes for breakfast are sometimes a good idea.

F **V** *4 portions*

Oats *help stabilise blood sugar and help to give long-lasting energy. They are also rich in a form of soluble fibre that protects intestinal surfaces and helps to keep the body's cholesterol levels down.*

SUPERFOODS

9 to 12 months:
growing independence

Your baby will probably be much more proficient at chewing and chopped or mashed food can replace purées. Many babies refuse to be spoon fed, so finger foods become an important part of the diet.

Moving on up

The final quarter of a baby's first year is a time of rapid change as babies will progress from sitting to crawling and maybe even walking. This is a time of growing independence and your baby will be delighted by this new freedom. During this stage, many babies refuse to be spoon-fed and only want to feed themselves. As your child's hand to eye co-ordination matures, he will find it much easier to feed himself and finger foods will become an increasingly important part of your baby's diet (see opposite).

Encourage your baby to experiment with using a spoon as soon as he is able to hold one. It will be messy at first and he may well end up biting the wrong end but eventually the food will actually reach its intended destination. The more you allow your baby to experiment, the quicker he will learn to feed himself. It is very important to encourage messy play with food as this enables learning of self-feeding and quicker development as well.

Learning to chew

By this age, your baby should have gained some teeth and graduated to a high chair so now it is important to introduce coarser textures in order to encourage your baby to chew. Your baby will gradually be eating more solids so that eventually solid food becomes the main part of the meal. Variety is important so try introducing lots of different flavours and textures during this stage. Try to give some food mashed, some grated, some diced and some whole. It is surprising what a few teeth and strong gums can get through.

Milk feeds

Your baby may be drinking less milk as her appetite for solid food increases, but she still needs 500–800 ml (17–28 fl oz) of her usual milk per day. Continue with breast, formula or follow-on milk until your baby is one year old as cow's milk is too low in iron and vitamin D. Milk is particularly important for calcium, which is necessary for developing bones and strong healthy teeth. Cow's

milk can be used with your baby's cereal or in other forms like cheese sauce or yoghurt.

If your baby wants extra drinks, offer boiled, cooled water. The sooner your baby can drink from a beaker, the better. There are lots of different beakers to choose from. A beaker with a long spout that is not rigid makes a good transition from a bottle. Aim to dispense with bottles by the age of one year. Most milk feeds are better given in a beaker or cup. If it helps to settle your baby, you can keep a breast or bottle-feed as a comfort before bedtime.

Which foods to choose

With the exception of raw or lightly cooked eggs, peanuts, whole nuts, shellfish and unpasteurised cheeses, your baby should now be able to eat most foods. At this age, your baby should be eating three to four servings of starchy food, three to four servings of fruit and vegetables, at least one serving of meat, chicken or fish, or two servings of a vegetable protein (soya, peas, beans, lentils and smooth nut butters) per day (see the food pyramid on page 15).

You can also now give wholegrain low-sugar adult breakfast cereals like Weetabix or Ready Brek and maybe add chopped fresh or dried fruits and some toasted wheatgerm for a nutritious breakfast. Eggs are also a good food for breakfast but you must make sure that the yolk and white are cooked until solid.

Your baby will probably also be following a more predictable sleeping pattern, which should help to make mealtimes more regular. Whenever possible let your baby sit in his high chair close to the table and enjoy eating with the rest of the family.

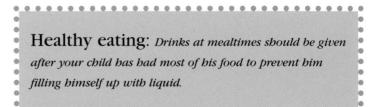

Healthy eating: *Drinks at mealtimes should be given after your child has had most of his food to prevent him filling himself up with liquid.*

Good foods for your baby

• Starchy foods including bread, pasta, rice, cereal and potato (can be of normal adult texture).

• Lean red meat – this provides the best source of iron.

• Calcium-rich foods like cheese, yoghurt – these are important for healthy bones and teeth.

• Eggs, these are a good source of protein.

• Plenty of fresh fruit and vegetables.

• Remember that babies need more of their diet to come from energy-rich fats and dairy products than adults do so give them foods like macaroni cheese, baked potato and cheese and rice pudding.

• Oily fish contain essential fatty acids that are very healthy. You could make salmon fishcakes with mashed potato, or mashed sardines (don't remove the soft bones, instead mash them in with the fish as this is a good source of calcium) and use them as a sandwich filling.

• If your child doesn't like eating meat, encourage her to eat other foods that are rich in iron like wholegrain cereals and bread, green leafy vegetables and pulses. Iron in foods of animal origin is much more easily absorbed but if you include a good source of vitamin C (e.g. kiwi fruit, orange juice) at the same meal, this will improve the absorption.

Foods to avoid

• Whole nuts.

• Salt or soy sauce.

• Artificial sweeteners.

• Added fibre in the form of bran, which can affect your baby's ability to absorb calcium, zinc and iron and other vitamins and minerals.

What to do if your baby chokes

If your baby chokes, do not try to fish the food from his mouth as you may only end up pushing it further down his throat. Tip him face-down over your lap with his head lower than his stomach and slap him firmly between the shoulder blades to dislodge the food.

Finger foods

As your baby develops better finger control (this usually happens at around eight months), introducing finger foods will help to develop the all-important skills of biting, chewing and self-feeding. Finger foods should be big enough for your baby to pick up, easy to hold and should not have any stones, pips or bones in them. You should also avoid small, hard foods like whole grapes that might cause your baby to choke. Just because your baby has teeth doesn't mean that she knows how to chew food. Instead, young babies are quite likely to bite off a piece of food, try to swallow it whole and choke on it (see box, above), so never leave a child alone while eating.

To begin with, as your baby learns to feed herself, she will probably drop a lot of her food on the floor. This can all seem very charming and amusing to begin with, but it can become a tragic waste of food. To prevent this happening, it's a good idea to invest in a plastic splash mat which can be laid under her high chair so that the food falls on a clean surface and can then be recycled. It will also ease the chore of clearing up behind her after every meal.

Tip: *Finger foods are great for occupying your child while you prepare his meal.*

Ideas for first finger foods

Offering a selection of these to your baby will get him used to chewing many different textures.

• Sticks of vegetables like carrots or parsnip make good finger food. But raw vegetables can be difficult to chew so it is much better to lightly steam vegetables or cook them in a little boiling water for a few minutes so that they are still crunchy but not quite so hard. When your baby seems to cope well with these, try introducing cucumber and as your baby gains more teeth, introduce raw vegetables like carrots.
• Fruits make good finger food and if your baby finds it difficult to chew, to begin with give soft fruits that melt in the mouth like banana, peach or kiwi fruit.
• Dried fruits like apricot or apple make good nutritious finger foods.
• Many babies who are teething really enjoy biting into something cold as it soothes the gums. A banana put into the freezer for a couple of hours makes an excellent teething aid (freeze the banana with the skin on), as does a chilled cucumber stick.
• Fingers of toast tend to work better than plain bread as they do not fall to pieces so readily.
• For fun finger food you can cut sandwiches, cheese or large vegetables into shapes using cookie cutters. Good sandwich fillings are mashed banana, cream cheese, egg mayonnaise (make sure it is pasteurised as homemade mayonnaises often contain raw egg yolk), Marmite or Promite, peanut butter, tuna and mayonnaise and hummus.
• Cooked pasta shapes.
• Rice cakes.
• Sticks of mild cheese.
• Goujons of fish or fish fingers.
• Slices or small chunks of chicken or turkey and miniature meatballs made of minced chicken, turkey, lamb or beef.

Equipment

This is a good time to invest in suction-based bowls and spill-proof cups. A splash mat (plastic sheet) under your child's chair will enable finger foods to be recycled. It can be a good idea to have two bowls of food, one for your baby to play with (preferably with a suction pad) and one from which you spoon feed your baby. You can expect a mess but you want to do your best to stop your child tipping his food on to the floor. A large wipe-clean bib will help to protect your baby's clothes.

Tip: *Don't expect your child to have good table manners at this age, exploring the feel of their food is all part of the learning process. The more you allow your child to experiment, the quicker he will get the hang of feeding himself.*

Meal planner

Other ideas for puddings are fresh fruit like a banana or grated apple, fruit purée and occasionally other desserts like ice cream, rice pudding, yoghurt and fromage frais.

	BREAKFAST	MID-MORNING	LUNCH	MID-AFTERNOON	SUPPER	BEDTIME
DAY 1	*Scrambled egg and toast* *Yoghurt*	*Breast or formula milk*	*Baby's Bolognese (p85)* *Fruit*	*Breast or formula milk*	*Mashed potato and carrot with broccoli and Gruyère (p74)* *Fruit*	*Breast or formula milk*
DAY 2	*My favourite porridge (p65)* *Fruit*	*Breast or formula milk*	*Yummy chicken with vegetables (p81)* *Fromage frais*	*Breast or formula milk*	*Tasty egg and tomato with cheese sauce (p78)* *Fresh peach melba (p85)*	*Breast or formula milk*
DAY 3	*Cereal* *Fruit*	*Breast or formula milk*	*Cherub's couscous (p78)* *Strawberry rice pudding (p86)*	*Breast or formula milk*	*Broccoli in cheese sauce (p75)* *Fruit*	*Breast or formula milk*
DAY 4	*French toast (p86)* *Fruit*	*Breast or formula milk*	*Mini-shepherd's pie (p83)* *First fruit purée (p40)*	*Breast or formula milk*	*Pasta risotto (p80)* *Strawberry and pear purée (p64)*	*Breast or formula milk*
DAY 5	*Cereal* *Apple, apricot and pear purée (p46)*	*Breast or formula milk*	*Tender chicken with fresh peach and pasta (p84)* *Fruit*	*Breast or formula milk*	*Fun finger foods with dips (p77)* *Strawberry rice pudding (p86)*	*Breast or formula milk*
DAY 6	*Scrambled egg and toast* *Fromage frais*	*Breast or formula milk*	*Carrot, cheese and tomato risotto (p74)* *Fresh peach melba (p85)*	*Breast or formula milk*	*Tender casserole of lamb (p84)* *Fruit*	*Breast or formula milk*
DAY 7	*Toast with yeast extract (Promite) or peanut butter* *Fruit*	*Breast or formula milk*	*Chopped chicken with diced vegetables (p80)* *Fruit*	*Breast or formula milk*	*Cheesy mushroom and tomato sauce with pasta (p75)* *Yoghurt*	*Breast or formula milk*

SUPERFOODS

Healthy eating:

Stronger-tasting vegetables like spinach are good combined with potato.

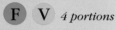 **F** **V** *4 portions*

Spinach *is rich in chlorophyll, the green pigment found in plants which helps prevent and treat anaemia. Spinach is a good source of betacarotene and vitamin C so do not overcook it or you will destroy a lot of its content. But despite popular opinion - and Popeye - it is not a particularly good source of iron.*

SUPERFOODS

Tiny pasta with Gruyère, spinach and sweetcorn

Spinach has quite a strong taste on its own, but blends well with a cheese sauce and the sweetcorn adds a slightly sweet taste that babies like. You can choose any tiny pasta shapes but I particularly like orzo, which is a pasta that looks like grains of rice.

3 tbsp orzo or other small pasta shapes
15 g (½ oz) unsalted butter
1 tbsp flour
150 ml (5 fl oz) your baby's usual milk
40 g (1½ oz) grated Gruyère cheese

85 g (3½ oz) fresh spinach (English spinach), tough stalks removed, or
40 g (½ oz) frozen spinach
40 g (1½ oz) cooked frozen sweetcorn

Cook the pasta according to the instructions on the packet. Melt the butter, stir in the flour and cook for 30 seconds. Gradually whisk in the milk to make a smooth white sauce. Bring to the boil and then simmer for 1 to 2 minutes. Remove from the heat and stir in the cheese until melted. If using fresh spinach carefully wash it and put in a saucepan, sprinkle with a little water and cook until tender (about 3 minutes). Squeeze out all the water. Combine the spinach (fresh or frozen) with the cheese sauce and purée in a mouli. Stir the cooked pasta and sweetcorn into the spinach and cheese sauce.

Spinach with mushrooms and potato

½ small onion, peeled and chopped
1 tbsp vegetable oil
100 g (4 oz) mushrooms, diced
250 g (9 oz) potatoes, peeled and diced
150 ml (5 fl oz) unsalted vegetable stock
100 g (4 oz) fresh spinach (English spinach), tough stalks removed, or
  50 g (2 oz) frozen spinach

Sauté the onion in the oil until softened. Add the mushrooms and sauté for 2 to 3 minutes. Add the potatoes and pour over the vegetable stock. Bring to the boil, then cover and simmer for 10 minutes. Add the spinach (carefully washed if fresh) and cook for 2 to 3 minutes. Mash with a fork or purée in a food processor.

SUPERFOODS

Broccoli *is king of the healthy vegetable superstars. Its phytochemicals have important properties, especially against cancer. It provides an excellent source of vitamin C and betacarotene. The darker the florets, the higher the amount of antioxidants. Broccoli should be steamed as boiling almost halves its vitamin C content.*

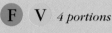

SUPERFOODS

Carrots *are more nutritious when cooked, unlike many other vegetables. Cooking breaks open the plant cells so antioxidants and other plant chemicals can be absorbed much better. Carrots contain large amounts of carotene, an antioxidant that gives it its orange colour.*

Mashed potato and carrot with broccoli and cheese

Mashing rather than puréeing your baby's food is a good way to gradually introduce more texture. Combining broccoli with creamy mashed potato and cheese is a great way to encourage babies to eat more greens.

150 g (5 oz) potatoes, peeled and diced
1 medium carrot, peeled and sliced
60 g (2½ oz) broccoli florets

4 tbsp your baby's usual milk
a knob of unsalted butter
25 g (1 oz) Gruyère or Cheddar cheese

Put the potatoes and carrots into a saucepan, cover with boiling water and cook until tender (about 20 minutes). Meanwhile, steam the broccoli until tender (about 8 minutes). Drain the potatoes and carrots and mash together with the broccoli, milk, butter and cheese.

Carrot, cheese and tomato risotto

This is a very easy to prepare and nutritious rice dish. Babies and toddlers tend to like rice and carrot and here I have flavoured them with sautéed tomatoes and melted cheese for a very tasty meal. Cooked rice is quite soft so is a good way of introducing texture to your baby's food.

25 g (1 oz) peeled and chopped onion
15 g (½ oz) unsalted butter
100 g (4 oz) long grain rice
150 g (5 oz) carrots, peeled and sliced
300 ml (10 fl oz) boiling water

3 tomatoes, skinned, de-seeded and chopped
50 g (2 oz) red Leicester cheese (Double Gloucester or medium Cheddar)

Sauté the onion in half the butter until softened. Stir in the rice until well coated, then add the carrot. Pour over the boiling water, bring back to the boil, then cover and simmer until the rice is cooked and the carrots are tender (15 to 20 minutes). If necessary, top up with extra water. Meanwhile, melt the remaining butter in a small pan, add the tomatoes and sauté until mushy (2 to 3 minutes). Stir in the cheese until melted. The water from the rice should have been absorbed but, if not, drain off any excess. Stir the tomato and cheese mixture into the cooked rice.

Cheesy mushroom and tomato sauce with pasta stars

The addition of tiny pasta shapes to this tasty tomato sauce enriched with mushrooms and cheese is a gentle way to introduce a little texture to your baby's food.

2 tbsp tiny pasta stars (or shapes)
25 g (1 oz) unsalted butter
½ small clove garlic
125 g (4½ oz) button mushrooms, sliced

3 tomatoes, skinned, de-seeded and
** roughly chopped**
25 g (1 oz) Cheddar cheese, grated

Cook the pasta according to the instructions on the packet. Melt the butter in a saucepan and sauté the garlic for about 30 seconds. Add the sliced mushrooms and sauté for 3 minutes. Add the tomatoes and cook, covered, until mushy (3 to 4 minutes). Stir in the cheese until melted. Purée the vegetable and cheese mixture, then stir in the cooked pasta.

Broccoli in cheese sauce

For older babies this also makes a good pasta sauce. Simply increase the amount of milk to 300 ml (10 fl oz) and add an extra 20 g (¾ oz) Gruyère cheese to the sauce and then mix with about 40 g (1½ oz) small pasta shapes. You could also make this with cauliflower.

100 g (4 oz) broccoli florets
20 g (¾ oz) unsalted butter
20 g (¾ oz) flour
250 ml (8 fl oz) your baby's usual milk

pinch of nutmeg
25 g (1 oz) Cheddar cheese, grated
25 g (1 oz) Gruyère cheese, grated

Steam the broccoli florets until tender (about 8 minutes). Alternatively, put in a saucepan, cover with boiling water and cook until tender. Meanwhile, to prepare the cheese sauce, melt the butter in a saucepan and stir in the flour to make a roux. Gradually whisk in the milk and the nutmeg to make a smooth white sauce. Bring to the boil and then simmer for 2 minutes. Remove from the heat and stir in the cheeses until melted. Chop the broccoli into small pieces and mix with the cheese sauce. Alternatively, purée the broccoli and cheese sauce.

 F **V** *3 portions*

SUPERFOODS

Tomatoes *contain lycopene, a powerful pigment important in the prevention of cancer. Men who have a high level of lycopene in their fat stores are half as likely to have a heart attack.*

Did you know?
Cosmetic companies are investigating tomatoes as sunscreens - chemicals in their skins may help prevent damage by ultraviolet rays.

F **V** *3 portions*

SUPERFOODS

Broccoli *eaten three times a week is believed to lower the risk of cancer. This is because broccoli contains glucosinolate, which triggers the production of cancer-fighting enzymes.*

Fun finger foods with dips

V *2 portions*

Once your baby is able to hold food, finger foods that allow your baby to feed herself will become an increasingly important part of her diet. Fresh fruit and vegetables served with tasty dips make an appealing and nutritious meal. Here are three of my favourites, each of which is particularly high-up on the SuperFood scale.

Creamy avocado dip

½ ripe avocado, mashed

2 tbsp cream cheese

1 tomato, skinned, de-seeded and chopped

1 tsp snipped chives (optional)

Mash the avocado together with the cream cheese and stir in the chopped tomato and snipped chives.

Serve with vegetables like carrots, cucumber, sweet pepper and celery. Give steamed vegetables to young babies and when they are better able to chew and swallow, move on to raw vegetables.

Cream cheese, tomato and chive dip

50 g (2 oz) cream cheese

3 tbsp crème fraîche

1 tsp tomato ketchup

1 tomato, skinned, de-seeded and chopped

1½ tsp snipped chives

Mix together the cream cheese, crème fraîche and tomato ketchup and stir in the chopped tomato and chives.

Raspberry yoghurt dip

100 g (4 oz) fresh or frozen raspberries

2 tbsp icing sugar

200 g (7 oz) Greek yoghurt

Purée the raspberries, press through a sieve and stir in the icing sugar. Stir the raspberry purée into the Greek yoghurt. Serve with fruits like strawberries, pear, apple and peach.

SUPERFOODS

Raspberries *are rich in vitamin C, which is needed for growth, healthy skin, bones and teeth and also helps the body to absorb iron from food. Raspberries are higher in folic acid and zinc than most fruits.*

Avocados *are sometimes thought of as a vegetable but they are actually a fruit and contain more nutrients than any other fruit. Avocados have the highest protein content of any fruit and are rich in monounsaturated fat, the 'good' type of fat, which helps prevent heart disease. The high calorie content of avocado makes them a good food for growing children.*

Tomatoes *are rich in lycopene (see page 75) and potassium, which is important for healthy blood and helps counteract the negative effect of salt. One of the factors of the good health of the Mediterranean people may be that their diet is rich in fruit and vegetables, including tomatoes.*

Tasty egg and tomato with cheese sauce

Eggs provide us with protein, vitamins and minerals, and egg yolk is a good source of iron, which is important for a baby's brain development. Raw or lightly cooked eggs should not be given to babies or young children because of the risk of salmonella. For babies under a year, cook the white and yolk until solid.

1 fresh egg

a knob of unsalted butter

1 tomato, skinned, de-seeded and roughly chopped

15 g (½ oz) Cheddar cheese, grated

Put the egg into a small saucepan, cover with water and bring to the boil. Boil the egg until the white and yolk are solid (about 10 minutes). Melt the butter in a small saucepan. Stir in the chopped tomato and cook until mushy (about 2 minutes). Remove from the heat and stir in the grated cheese until melted. Remove the shell from the egg and mash with a fork. Mix with the tomato and cheese.

Cherub's couscous

250 ml (8 fl oz) unsalted chicken stock

100 g (4 oz) couscous

15 g (½ oz) unsalted butter

25 g (1 oz) peeled and chopped onion

50 g (2 oz) courgettes (zucchini), washed and diced

2 tomatoes, skinned, de-seeded and chopped

50 g (2 oz) cooked chicken, diced

Bring the chicken stock to the boil and pour over the couscous, stir with a fork and set aside for 6 minutes, by which time it will have absorbed the stock. Meanwhile, melt the butter in a saucepan and sauté the onion for 2 minutes. Add the courgettes and sauté for about 4 minutes, then add the tomatoes and cook for 1 minute. Fluff the couscous with a fork and mix in the courgettes and tomato mixture together with the chicken.

Chopped chicken with diced vegetables in cheese sauce

Combining finely chopped food with a creamy cheese sauce makes lumpier textures easier to swallow. If you don't have any cooked chicken, you could poach 50 g (2 oz) raw chicken in stock for about 10 minutes. You could also use flaked fish instead of the cooked chicken.

50 g (2 oz) broccoli florets
50 g (2 oz) carrots, peeled and sliced
25 g (1 oz) unsalted butter
2 tbsp flour

250 ml (8 fl oz) your baby's usual milk
40 g (1½ oz) Edam or Cheddar cheese, grated
50 g (2 oz) cooked chicken, diced

Steam the broccoli and carrots until tender. Cut the broccoli into small pieces and dice the carrot. To prepare the cheese sauce, melt the butter in a saucepan, stir in the flour and cook for 1 minute. Gradually whisk in the milk, bring to the boil and cook until the sauce has thickened. Remove from the heat and stir in the cheese until melted. Mix the cooked chicken and vegetables into the cheese sauce. For young babies, purée to the desired consistency in a blender.

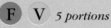
Pasta risotto

You can vary the vegetables in this tasty and simple to prepare recipe. Try also peas, sweetcorn or diced tomatoes.

75 g (3 oz) orzo or other small pasta shapes
50 g (2 oz) carrots, peeled and diced
50 g (2 oz) courgettes (zucchini), washed and diced

50 g (2 oz) broccoli florets, diced
25 g (1 oz) unsalted butter
25 g (1 oz) Cheddar cheese, grated

Put the pasta in a saucepan together with the carrots, cover generously with boiling water and cook for 5 minutes. Add the broccoli and courgettes and continue to cook for about 7 minutes. Melt the butter in a saucepan, stir in the drained pasta and vegetables and toss with the butter and Cheddar cheese until the cheese has melted.

Orzo with creamy mushroom and cheese sauce

175 g (6 oz) orzo or other small pasta shapes

25 g (1 oz) peeled and chopped onion

25 g (1 oz) red pepper (capsicum), de-seeded and diced

1 tbsp olive oil

85 g (3½ oz) button mushrooms, diced

20 g (¾ oz) unsalted butter

1 tbsp flour

175 ml (6 fl oz) your baby's usual milk

20 g (¾ oz) Parmesan cheese, grated

Cook the orzo in a pan of boiling water according to the packet instructions and drain. Meanwhile, sauté the onion and red pepper in the olive oil until softened (about 5 minutes). Add the diced mushrooms and sauté for 2 to 3 minutes.

To make the cheese sauce, melt the butter in a small saucepan and stir in the flour to make a roux. Gradually whisk in the milk over a medium heat until the sauce has thickened and finally stir in the cheese. To serve, simply mix together the orzo, vegetables and cheese sauce.

Risotto with butternut squash

Cooked rice with vegetables is nice and soft so it's a good way to introduce texture to your baby's food. Butternut squash is now more readily available in supermarkets and it is rich in vitamin A. You could also make this with pumpkin instead of squash.

50 g (2 oz) onion, chopped

25 g (1 oz) butter

100 g (4 oz) basmati rice

150 g (5 oz) chopped, peeled butternut squash

450 ml (1 pint) boiling water

3 ripe tomatoes (approx. 225 g/8 oz), skinned, de-seeded and chopped

50 g (2 oz) Cheddar cheese, grated

Sauté the onion in half the butter until softened. Stir in the rice until well coated. Pour over the boiling water, cover and cook for 8 minutes over a high heat. Stir in the chopped butternut squash, reduce the heat and cook, covered, for about 12 minutes or until the water has been absorbed.

Meanwhile, melt the remaining butter in a small pan, add the chopped tomatoes and sauté for 2 to 3 minutes. Stir in the cheese until melted.

F **V** *5 portions*

Cheese *is a perfect food for children. It provides an excellent source of protein and calcium, important for strong bones and good teeth.*

Healthy eating:
For older children you could serve this dish with some freshly grated Parmesan cheese sprinkled on top.

F *4 portions*

Butternut squash *is rich in betacarotene, the plant form of vitamin A, which helps protect against cancer and boosts your child's immune system.*

SUPERFOODS

SUPERFOODS

Mini-shepherd's pie

Combining minced meat with creamy mashed potato gives it a much smoother texture that is easier to swallow. Mashed potatoes and carrots or mashed potatoes and swede makes a tasty combination and combines well with minced meat. For babies under nine months it would be best to purée the minced meat before combining it with the mashed potato.

300 g (10 oz) potatoes, peeled and diced
100 g (4 oz) carrots, peeled and sliced
1 tbsp vegetable oil
25 g (1 oz) peeled and chopped onion
100 g (4 oz) lean minced beef or lamb
1 tomato, skinned, de-seeded and chopped
1 tsp tomato ketchup
150 ml (5 fl oz) unsalted chicken stock
15 g (½ oz) unsalted butter
2 tbsp your baby's usual milk

Put the potatoes and carrots into a saucepan, pour over boiling water and cook the vegetables until tender (about 20 minutes). Meanwhile, heat the vegetable oil in a small saucepan and sauté the onion until softened. Add the minced meat and sauté, stirring occasionally, until browned all over. Add the chopped tomato and ketchup and pour over the stock. Cover, bring to the boil and then simmer for about 20 minutes. When the potatoes and carrots are cooked, drain them and return to the saucepan together with the butter and milk, and mash with a potato masher or potato ricer until smooth. Mix the minced meat with the mashed potato and carrot.

For young babies, purée the minced meat in a food processor before mixing it with the mashed potato and carrot. As your baby gets a little older make this into a mini-shepherd's pie and decorate with a face made from vegetables.

F *2 portions*

Red meat *provides a rich source of iron and by including it with foods like dark green leafy vegetables or wholemeal bread you will improve the absorption of the vegetable sources of iron by three times.*

SUPERFOODS

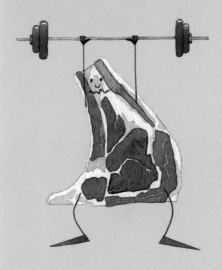

Finger-picking chicken balls

These tasty chicken balls make great finger food.

1 onion, finely chopped
50 g (2 oz) grated carrot
1 tbsp light olive oil
1 large Granny Smith apple, peeled and
    grated
2 chicken breasts (350 g/12 oz), cut into
    chunks

1 tbsp parsley
1 tsp fresh or $\frac{1}{2}$ tsp dried thyme
    (optional)
50 g (2 oz) fresh white breadcrumbs
1 chicken stock cube, crumbled
flour for coating
vegetable oil for frying

Heat the oil in a pan and sauté half the onion and the grated carrot for 3 minutes, stirring occasionally. Using your hands, squeeze out a little excess liquid from the grated apple. Mix together the grated apple, chicken, onion and carrot plus raw chopped onion, parsley and thyme (if using), breadcrumbs and crumbled stock cube and chop for a few seconds in a food processor. Season with a little salt and pepper.

   With your hands, form the mixture into about 20 balls, roll in flour and fry in shallow oil until lightly golden and cooked through (about 4 to 5 minutes).

Tender casserole of lamb

Cooking lamb in a casserole with vegetables such as carrots, potatoes and tomatoes and stock makes it tender and moist for your baby.

2 lamb cutlets (approximately 160 g/5$\frac{1}{2}$ oz)
$\frac{1}{2}$ small onion, peeled and chopped
200 g (7 oz) potatoes, peeled and diced
100 g (4 oz) carrots, peeled and sliced
2 tomatoes, skinned, de-seeded and chopped
125 ml (4 fl oz) unsalted chicken stock

Pre-heat an oven to 180°C/350°F/Gas Mark 4. Put the lamb cutlets, vegetables and stock into a small casserole, cover and cook until the lamb is tender (about 1 hour). Chop into small pieces or purée for young babies.

Baby's Bolognese

Often it is not the taste of red meat that babies dislike but the texture, so here I blend the minced meat so that it becomes very easy to chew. I then mix it with soft pasta.

1 tbsp vegetable oil
25 g (1 oz) peeled and finely chopped onion
15 g (½ oz) celery, finely chopped
25 g (1 oz) finely grated carrot
125 g (4½ oz) lean minced beef
1 tbsp tomato ketchup
2 tomatoes, skinned, de-seeded and chopped
100 ml (3 fl oz) unsalted chicken stock
40 g (1½ oz) spaghetti

Sauté the onion and celery in the vegetable oil for 3 to 4 minutes. Add the grated carrot and cook for 2 minutes. Add the minced beef and stir until browned. Stir in the tomato ketchup, tomatoes and stock. Bring the mixture to the boil, then reduce the heat, cover and cook until the meat is cooked through (10 to 15 minutes). Meanwhile, cook the spaghetti until quite soft. Drain and chop into short lengths. Transfer the Bolognese sauce to a food processor and purée to a fairly smooth texture before combining with the pasta.

Fresh peach melba

This raspberry sauce is also good served with fresh strawberries.

100 g (4 oz) fresh or defrosted frozen raspberries
1 tbsp icing sugar
2 scoops vanilla ice cream
2 ripe peaches, peeled, stoned and sliced

Make the melba sauce by puréeing the raspberries in a food processor, then push them through a sieve to get rid of the seeds and stir in the icing sugar until dissolved. Put the ice cream into a dish together with the peach slices and pour the sauce over the top.

 5 portions

Red meat *provides most nutritional needs apart from fibre. It is an excellent source of iron. Iron deficiency is the commonest nutritional deficiency in early childhood and leads to a serious medical condition called anaemia if left unchecked. A baby's iron reserves inherited from his mother run out around the age of six months, so it is important to include in the diet foods rich in iron.*

SUPERFOODS

2 portions

Raspberries *that are frozen are just as nutritious as fresh. Eating raspberries can increase resistance to and inhibit the growth of cancer cells because they contain ellagic acid, which is an anti-carcinogen.*

SUPERFOODS

5 portions

SUPERFOODS

Milk *provides an excellent source of protein for growth and calcium, which is important for healthy bones and teeth.*

1 to 2 portions

SUPERFOODS

Breads *are now available in a staggering variety. When choosing bread, choose ones that are made from wholemeal or whole grains. These breads contain all the goodness of the complete wheat husk and wheatgerm, are higher in fibre and a good source of B vitamins. Brown and white breads have had a lot of goodness leached from them in the processing.*

Strawberry rice pudding

The secret of a good rice pudding is long, slow cooking. You could leave out the strawberry jam and add some cooked fruit like stewed plums or add some chopped dried fruits instead like semi-dried mango or dried apricots, which can be cooked together with the rice.

50 g (2 oz) pudding rice
600 ml (1 pint) your baby's usual milk
¼ tsp vanilla essence
1½ tbsp caster sugar
knob of unsalted butter
strawberry jam

Pre-heat an oven to 150°C/300°F/Gas Mark 2. Place the rice, milk, vanilla and sugar in a greased ovenproof dish and stir well. Dot the surface with butter. Bake for 30 minutes, then stir the rice. Continue to bake until the rice is tender (1 to 1½ hours). Remove from the oven and serve each portion topped with strawberry jam.

French toast

1 or 2 slices white bread, raisin bread or use slices of French bread
Marmite or Promite (optional)
1 egg
2 tbsp full-fat milk
a generous knob of unsalted butter and a little vegetable oil
sugar and/or cinnamon (optional)

If using sliced bread, remove the crusts and cut into four triangles or into fingers. If you would like a savoury version, spread a thin layer of Marmite on the bread. Beat together the egg and milk and soak the bread in this mixture for a few seconds. Drain on kitchen paper. Heat the butter or oil in a frying pan and fry until brown on both sides.

For a sweet version, add a little sugar or a pinch of ground cinnamon to the egg mixture and sprinkle a little sugar on to the toast after frying.

1 to 2 years:

time to explore

From the age of one, solid food will replace much of the milk in your baby's diet. Try introducing a wider variety of foods, presented in an appealing way, and encourage your baby to feed himself.

Breakfast power

There is a lot of truth in that old saying 'Breakfast like a king, lunch like a knave and dine like a pauper'. However, up to 17 per cent of school children skip breakfast before school. The first meal of the day is the most important as your child will probably have fasted for up to 12 hours. Our bodies release glucose from our stores shortly before we wake up to help us arise from bed. Once awake, the glucose needs to be replaced by food in order to give your child's brain a kick start. Improving blood sugar by eating a good breakfast after the night's fast raises blood glucose ('fuel for the brain') and will help to improve your child's performance. Recent research has shown that 'children who eat a nutritionally balanced breakfast worked faster, made significantly fewer mistakes on tasks requiring sustained attention, demonstrated greater physical endurance and appeared less tired to teachers'. Studies have also shown that children who go to school on a good breakfast will not only concentrate better but will also be better able to remember what they are taught.

No one really needs scientists to tell them that it is easier to focus on a mental task if their tummy is not rumbling with hunger. Breakfast sets the pattern for healthy eating during the day and if your child misses breakfast, he will end up craving sweet foods later in the morning because his body will need glucose fast. Breakfast is the ideal time to make sure that your child gets some healthy energy giving food into his diet as, unlike school lunch, you are in control of what your child eats. My favourite ways of serving delicious breakfasts are given here.

Breakfasts for energy and brain power

Children have high energy and nutrient requirements because they are active and growing rapidly so it is important that their diet is not too high in fibre or low in fat, otherwise your child may feel full before his requirements are met. Choose whole milk and whole milk dairy products and don't give too many high-fibre cereals.

For toddlers, especially, it is important to remember that little people have small stomachs that get full quickly. The food they eat needs to be packed full of as many nutrients as possible. Peanut butter on toast, a yoghurt or some cheese and a glass of fruit juice would provide an excellent breakfast for a toddler. Eggs are good for breakfast and very versatile. Baked beans on toast is another simple way to kick-start the day.

While children are still growing, it is important that they get a good supply of vital nutrients like calcium and iron. Children who eat a good breakfast are much less likely to suffer nutritional deficiencies. After all, a simple bowl of cereal with milk will supply both iron and calcium.

For maximum energy and brain power to last throughout the morning a good breakfast should ideally include something from each of these groups:

- Complex carbohydrate: cereal and bread.
- Protein: dairy products, eggs and nuts.
- Vitamins and minerals: fruit (occasionally vegetables, as in an omelette).

Calcium

Try to include at least one calcium-rich food each day for breakfast (see the meal planner on page 93). A good supply of calcium is essential to ensure the development of strong, healthy bones and this is particularly important during childhood and the teenage years when there is rapid growth. Calcium is also essential for the development of teeth, being a key part of the tooth structure. Milk and dairy products are the main source of calcium in our diet. (See also page 14.)

Eggs

Eggs are rich in essential nutrients and almost all the nutrients are concentrated in the yolk, which contains protein, fat, vitamins, minerals and folic acid. Eggs are a good source of iron.

Very young children should not eat lightly cooked or raw eggs because of the risk of salmonella. Very fresh eggs contain fewer bacteria than older eggs so try to find eggs that display the date on which they were laid.

The importance of iron

Iron deficiency is the commonest nutritional deficiency in young children. Recent surveys have shown that one in every five babies aged 10 to 12 months has daily intakes of iron below the recommended level. Two of the main symptoms are tiredness and lack of concentration. Fortified cereals and wholemeal bread are good sources of iron. But to improve the absorption of the iron you will need to include vitamin C-rich fruit like kiwi or berry fruits or vitamin C-rich juice like orange juice or cranberry juice. (See also page 17.)

Bread and cereals

A bowl of cereal can make a healthy start to the day but you will need to choose carefully. Many of the attractively packaged breakfast cereals designed specifically for children are highly refined and have lost most of their valuable nutrients. Don't be misled by claims that they are fortified with important vitamins and minerals since many more nutrients are taken out than put back. These cereals also tend to be very high in sugar (sometimes nearly 50 per cent sugar). Not only are these bad for children's teeth, but the high level of sugar can cause blood sugar levels to rise quickly and then fall, leaving your child feeling tired and listless.

In an ideal world it would be best for our children to eat wholegrain cereals like muesli, porridge and wholegrain or wholemeal bread, but even if your child is hooked on sugary cereals, she's still getting calcium from the milk she adds to the cereal (sugary cereals contain lots of carbohydrate). You might find that mixing sugary cereals with wholegrain cereals makes a good compromise. You can also boost the nutrition in a bowl of cereal by adding fresh or dried fruits or try sprinkling cereals with wheatgerm.

Healthy eating: *Chubby babies at the age of one soon slim down once they start walking.*

Fruit

Breakfast provides a good opportunity to eat some fresh fruit towards the recommended five portions of fruit and vegetables each day. Different fruits contain different vitamins so try to include plenty of variety. Think of different ways of presenting fruit like a two-colour fruit salad, or cut a kiwi in half, serve it in an egg cup and let your child scoop out the flesh with a teaspoon. Fruity milkshakes are another way to encourage your child to consume more fruit, or make fruit smoothies, mango, strawberry, banana and fresh orange juice makes a delicious combination.

Helping fussy children

Babies grow more rapidly in their first year than at any other time in their lives, but after twelve months, a child's growth and weight-gain generally slow down. It is not so surprising, therefore, that many children who were good eaters in their first year become more fussy and the second year is often a time when food is used to assert independence.

Once your child starts to walk and to get around by himself, his life becomes much more interesting. It is not surprising therefore that many toddlers lose interest in food around this stage and would much rather play with their toys and run around. However unreasonable your child's eating habits, try to respond calmly. Food shouldn't be used as a means to teach a child to do as he is told. If your child refuses his meal, don't make a fuss but leave the meal in front of him, and carry on eating your own meal. He will soon realise that refusing food isn't much fun when you don't react and he doesn't get the attention he is looking for. You need to be firm and consistent and try to make mealtimes enjoyable. Introduce your baby to a wide variety of foods; it's surprising how sophisticated their tastes can be at a very early age. Allow your child to taste food from your plate – someone else's food is often more tempting. Give your child lots of praise when he tries a new food.

Top tips for coping with fussy eaters

• The first thing to do when trying to help your child overcome fussy eating habits is to only buy the foods that you want your child to eat. You should also set an example by eating the right foods yourself.

• If your child doesn't like eating vegetables, try to disguise them by blending them into a tomato sauce for pasta or adding vegetables to a pizza topping. Also, many children who don't like eating cooked vegetables do like eating them raw, so give carrot sticks, cucumber, sweet pepper (capsicum), etc. with a tasty dip.

• Red meat is good for children as it provides the best source of iron. It is often the texture rather than the taste of meat that children object to. To make meat easier to chew, cook minced meat and chop it in a food processor for a few seconds and then make it into dishes like spaghetti Bolognese, lasagne or shepherd's pie.

• Many children have a poor appetite at mealtimes because they have so many in-between snacks that they never feel truly hungry. Cut out empty calories like crisps, sweet biscuits and soft drinks and replace them with snacks that are nutritious, like fresh fruit, cheese or raw vegetables.

• Don't put too much food on your child's plate. Try to make food look attractive and fun, simple things like eating half a kiwi in an egg cup or cutting sandwiches into shapes using cookie cutters.

• Make mealtimes into an occasion; children who eat sitting at the table with other people are more likely to eat well and be less fussy. Avoid distractions like television at mealtimes.

• If your child refuses to eat, simply remove his plate and offer nothing until the next mealtime.

Your baby's milk

At one year, children can switch from formula or breast milk to whole cow's milk. The iron in breast milk is easily absorbed and infant formulas also contain good quantities of iron. Cow's milk, however, is a poor source of iron and can also block iron absorption if given as part of a meal, so make sure that your child gets plenty of iron in her daily diet in other ways (see page 17).

From one year your child needs about 400 ml (14 fl oz) of milk a day but give full-fat cow's milk and not semi-skimmed milk before the age of two as it is low in energy that your child needs to grow. For very picky eaters there may be advantages in continuing with a follow-on formula (which is fortified with vitamins and iron) until two years of age. Yogurts, fromage frais or pasteurised cheese can be used as equivalents to milk and you can smuggle milk into recipes like cauliflower cheese or rice pudding.

Family cuisine

Life is too short to cook a different meal for every member of the family. At this age, toddlers can eat almost everything that adult members of the family eat, with the exception of whole nuts, unpasteurised soft cheeses and lightly cooked eggs. This is a good time to review your family's eating habits as it is important to set up a healthy eating pattern for your child very early on, rather than wait till they are three or four when they already have strong likes and dislikes. It is great if children can eat regularly with the rest of the family where they can see a selection of foods being enjoyed.

Attractive presentation will help to make a meal appealing to a toddler. Without going to extremes, bright colours and interesting shapes can go a long way to stimulating a reluctant appetite. If you are making a recipe for the whole family, such as a shepherd's pie, it is much more attractive to prepare a mini-portion in a small dish like a ramekin rather than dollop a spoonful on to your child's plate. It can save time to plan ahead and when cooking a recipe, make several small portions that can be frozen for future use. Most of the recipes in this book are suitable for freezing and this is always indicated by the symbol F next to relevant recipes.

Meal planner

	BREAKFAST	LUNCH	SUPPER
DAY 1	Cereal *Peach melba smoothie (p111)*	*Rice 'n' easy (p106)* *Peach, strawberry and raspberry ice lolly (block) (p108)*	*Home-made cream of tomato soup (p94)* *Baked potato* *Fruit*
DAY 2	*French toast (p86)* *Fruit*	*Scarlett's spaghetti Bolognese (p104)* *Fruit*	*Rabbit muffins (p94)* *Yoghurt and honey*
DAY 3	*Porridge* *Yoghurt*	*Orzo risotto (p96)* *Fruit and ice cream*	*Mini-fish pie (p105)* *Vegetables* *Fruit*
DAY 4	*Scrambled egg and toast* *Fruit*	*Meatballs with sweet and sour sauce (p102) and Chinese fried rice (p123)* *Lara's luscious lychee ice lolly (block) (p108)*	*Tasty brown rice with lentils (p97)* *Fun ways with fruit (p108)*
DAY 5	*Cereal* *Peach melba smoothie (p111)*	*Annabel's tasty chicken skewers (p101)* *Rice and vegetables* *Summer fruit brulée (p111)*	*Tomato sauce with hidden vegetables and pasta (p99)* *Fruit*
DAY 6	*Cheese on toast* *Fruit*	*Fillet of fish with herb butter (p104) with vegetables and chips* *Fruit*	*Carrot soup with yellow split peas (p96)* *Baked potato* *Fresh peach melba (p85)*
DAY 7	*Scrambled egg and toast* *Fruit*	*Cheese and sweetcorn pancakes (p100)* *Fruit*	*Chicken with matchsticks (p100)* *Peach, strawberry and raspberry ice lolly (block) (p108)*

Three servings of dairy products should be included daily, e.g. cheese, yoghurt or a milky drink.

Cheese *is high in saturated fat, which is not good for adults but is a great energy food for children. Cheese is also a good source of riboflavin (vitamin B2), which is essential for converting proteins, fats and carbohydrates into energy. Cheese is a good source of vitamin B12 for people who don't eat meat.*

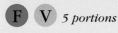 *5 portions*

Tomatoes *are an excellent source of lycopene, an antioxidant pigment that helps to prevent cancer and heart disease. However, research shows that lycopene in tomatoes can be absorbed more efficiently by the body if the tomatoes have been cooked with a little oil.*

Rabbit muffins

a knob of butter
1 spring onion, finely chopped
50 g (2 oz) Cheddar cheese, grated
1 wholemeal muffin, split in half
1 tbsp good quality tomato sauce

DECORATION
1 carrot
1 black olive
frozen peas
sweetcorn
salad cress

Melt the butter and sauté the spring onion until softened. Stir in the grated cheese until melted. Toast the muffins and divide the tomato sauce between them, then cover with the cheese sauce. Cook under a pre-heated grill until golden (about 2 minutes). If you like, decorate the muffins to look like rabbits.

Home-made cream of tomato soup

Some children don't like green bits floating around in their soup so you can leave out the basil if your child prefers.

1½ tbsp olive oil
1 onion, peeled and chopped
1 clove garlic, crushed
175 g (6 oz) carrots, peeled and sliced
1 medium potato, peeled and diced
1 x 400 g (14 oz) can chopped tomatoes
500 g (1 lb 2 oz) plum tomatoes, skinned, de-seeded and chopped

1 tbsp tomato purée (paste)
¼ tsp caster sugar
425 ml (15 fl oz) chicken or vegetable stock
freshly ground black pepper
3 tbsp double (thickened) cream (optional)
2 tbsp torn fresh basil leaves (optional)

Warm the olive oil in a large pan over a low heat, then add the onion and garlic and sauté for 2 to 3 minutes. Add the carrots and potatoes and sauté for about 8 minutes. Add the remaining ingredients, apart from the cream and basil (if using). Bring to the boil, then cover and simmer for about 30 minutes. Liquidise until smooth and press through a sieve. Add the cream and basil and reheat, but do not bring to the boil.

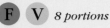

F V *8 portions*

Carrots *do improve night vision. They are an excellent source of betacarotene, which is formed in the body into vitamin A and one of the first symptoms of vitamin A deficiency is night blindness.*

Carrot soup with yellow split peas

This soup is packed full of nutrient and is a good source of protein for vegetarians.

225 g (8 oz) split yellow peas
25 g (1 oz) butter
350 g (12 oz) carrots, peeled and sliced
1 onion, peeled and chopped
1 bay leaf
1 clove garlic, crushed

100 g (4 oz) washed and sliced leeks
1.2 litres (2 pints) vegetable stock
2 tbsp crème fraîche
1 tbsp fresh chopped parsley, salt and freshly ground black pepper

Soak the split peas in cold water overnight. Melt the butter in a large saucepan and sauté the carrots, onion, bay leaf and garlic for 3 to 4 minutes. Stir in the leek and split peas. Pour in the vegetable stock, cover and bring to the boil and simmer for 40 minutes. Remove the bay leaf and liquidise in a food processor. Stir in the crème fraîche and parsley and season to taste.

V *6 portions*

Pasta *is a good source of complex carbohydrate, which provides us with sustained energy. This is why it is so popular with sportsmen. Try mixing some wholemeal pasta with regular pasta to increase the fibre content of the meal.*

Did you know?

Sixty per cent of the energy in an adult's diet should come from carbohydrates.

Orzo risotto

1 tbsp olive oil
25 g (1 oz) butter
2 onions, peeled and finely chopped
1 clove garlic, crushed
100 g (4 oz) courgettes (zucchini), washed and diced
100 g (4 oz) red/yellow pepper (capsicum), de-seeded and diced
100 g (4 oz) button mushrooms, diced

300 g (10 oz) orzo or other small pasta shapes
1 tsp fresh thyme, finely chopped
1 bay leaf
1.3 litres (2 pints) chicken or vegetable stock
4 tbsp freshly grated Parmesan cheese
salt and freshly ground black pepper

Heat the oil and a small knob of butter from the 25 g (1 oz) butter. Sauté the onions, garlic and courgettes for 5 minutes. Stir in the pepper and mushrooms for 2 minutes. Stir in the orzo, thyme, bay leaf and about a quarter of the stock and cook over a low heat until the stock is almost absorbed, stirring frequently. Gradually add the rest of the stock, waiting each time until almost all the liquid has been absorbed. This will take about 20 minutes. Remove the bay leaf and stir in the remaining butter and the Parmesan cheese. Season to taste.

Tasty brown rice with lentils

F V *6 portions*

Personally, I have always liked the nutty taste of brown rice and it is so much more nutritious than refined white rice. Brown rice has a very low allergy risk, which makes it ideal for small children. Adding lentils and vegetables makes this a meal in itself and is perfect for vegetarians.

1 tbsp olive oil

25 g (1 oz) butter

1 red onion, peeled and chopped

1 clove garlic, crushed

½ red pepper (capsicum), cored, de-seeded and diced

150 g (5 oz) button mushrooms, sliced

125 g (4½ oz) brown, green or red lentils

600 ml (1 pint) vegetable stock

150 g (5 oz) brown long-grain rice

150 g (5 oz) fresh baby leaf spinach (English spinach), washed

3 tomatoes, skinned, de-seeded and roughly chopped

1½ tsp lemon juice

1 tbsp fresh chopped parsley

salt and freshly ground black pepper

Heat the oil and butter in a large saucepan and sauté the onion, garlic and pepper for 5 minutes. Stir in the mushrooms and lentils. Sauté for 1 to 2 minutes, stirring continuously, and then pour over the vegetable stock. Cover with a lid and cook for 10 minutes. Remove the lid and stir in the rice. Cover and cook for 35 minutes, stirring occasionally and adding any extra stock if needed. Remove the lid and stir in the spinach, tomatoes, lemon juice and parsley, and cook for two minutes. Season with salt and pepper.

Lentils *feature high up on the list of SuperFoods and contain properties that can help reduce the risk of developing heart disease and cancer. They are an excellent source of protein, iron, selenium and potassium.*

SUPERFOODS

Healthy eating:

There is always some nutrient loss when vegetables are cooked, particularly the water-soluble vitamins B and C. However, when vegetables are cooked in stock to make soup, the liquid absorbs the water-soluble vitamins and as we end up consuming both the liquid and the vegetables, more of the original nutrient content is retained.

Tomato sauce with hidden vegetables

This is a delicious tomato sauce flavoured with a hint of creamy mascarpone cheese. This is a great way to get children to eat vegetables because this sauce makes them invisible and what they can't see, they can't pick out. Serve with the pasta of your choice.

1 tbsp vegetable oil
1 onion, peeled and chopped
1 clove garlic, crushed
75 g (3 oz) carrots, peeled and sliced
½ red pepper (capsicum), de-seeded and diced
100 g (4 oz) courgettes (zucchini), washed and diced
25 g (1 oz) butter
½ leek, washed and sliced
75 g (3 oz) mushrooms, chopped
3 plum tomatoes, skinned, de-seeded and chopped
400 ml (14 fl oz) passata (tomato purée)
1 tbsp fresh basil leaves
1 tbsp fresh parsley, chopped
a pinch of sugar
salt and freshly ground black pepper
50 g (2 oz) mascarpone cheese
250 g (9 oz) pasta shapes

Sauté the onion and garlic in the oil until beginning to soften (about 2 minutes). Add the carrots and sauté for 4 minutes. Add the red pepper and courgettes and sauté until beginning to soften (2 to 3 minutes). Add the butter, leek and mushrooms and cook for 5 minutes. Add the tomatoes, passata, basil, parsley, sugar and salt and pepper and simmer, covered, for 15 minutes. Blend in a food processor. Press through a sieve and stir in the mascarpone cheese.

Meanwhile, cook the pasta according to the packet instructions. When it's cooked, drain in a colander and toss with the tomato sauce.

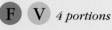

F V *4 portions*

Brightly coloured vegetables *contain a wide variety of phytochemicals (plant chemicals) that will give us a higher chance of preventing diseases such as coronary heart disease and cancer. Tinned tomatoes and passata retain most of their nutrients but do also contain salt.*

SUPERFOODS

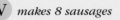

SUPERFOODS

Cheese *is particularly beneficial at the end of a meal as it raises the calcium concentration in plaque. Protein from cheese is also absorbed onto the enamel surface and physically slows down dental caries.*

F *4 portions*

SUPERFOODS

Chicken *contains much less fat than other meats as most of the fat lies in the skin which can be removed. However, chicken with the skin on is higher in fat than beef and other red meats.*

Cheese and courgette sausages

Delicious vegetarian sausages that are quick and easy to prepare. If you have time you can form the mixture into sausage shapes and then set aside in the fridge to firm up before frying.

175 g (6 oz) sliced white bread
25 g (1 oz) butter
1 medium onion, finely chopped
175 g (6 oz) grated courgette

150 g (5 oz) Cheddar cheese, grated
1 egg, separated
a little salt and pepper
oil for frying

Make the breadcrumbs by tearing the bread into pieces and blitzing it in a food processor

Heat the butter in a frying pan and fry the onion until soft. Add the grated courgette and cook for 3 minutes until softened.

Mix with the grated cheese, half the breadcrumbs, the egg yolk and seasoning. Shape into 8 sausages about 10 cm (4 in) long, using floured hands. Dip into the lightly beaten egg white and then roll in the remaining breadcrumbs.

Heat some oil in a wok or frying pan and shallow-fry the sausages until lightly golden.

Chicken with matchsticks

This is quick and easy to prepare and everything is cut into little bite-sized pieces perfect for a one-year-old. As a special treat you can buy child-friendly plastic chopsticks, which are joined at the top and can be used by children as young as two. Serve with rice.

SAUCE
2 tsp red wine vinegar
2 tbsp soy sauce
2 tbsp tomato ketchup
2 tbsp olive oil
4 tbsp pineapple juice
2 tsp sugar

2 chicken breasts
salt and freshly ground black pepper
1½ tbsp vegetable oil
40 g (1½ oz) carrot matchsticks
40 g (1½ oz) courgette (zucchini) matchsticks (unpeeled)
40 g (1½ oz) baby sweetcorn, sliced in half lengthways

Mix together all the ingredients for the sauce and set aside. Cut the chicken breasts into strips, season them with a little salt and pepper and sauté until cooked through (4 to 5 minutes). Drain on kitchen paper. Steam the carrot, courgette and baby sweetcorn for about 4 minutes so that they are cooked but still crunchy. Bring the sauce to the boil, simmer for about a minute and stir in the vegetable strips and chicken.

Annabel's tasty chicken skewers

Marinated chicken skewers make an easy-to-prepare and very tasty meal. They can also be cooked on the barbecue.

2 chicken breasts, cut into chunks
2 tbsp soy sauce
20 g (¾ oz) light muscovado (light brown) sugar
½ tbsp lime or lemon juice
½ tbsp vegetable oil
½ small garlic clove, crushed

Put the soy sauce and sugar into a small saucepan and gently heat until the sugar has dissolved. Remove from the heat, stir in the lime or lemon juice, vegetable oil and garlic. Allow the marinade to cool for a few minutes and then marinate the chicken for at least 1 hour or overnight. Soak four bamboo skewers in water to prevent them from getting scorched. Pre-heat the oven to 180°C/350°F/Gas Mark 4. Thread the chunks of chicken on to the skewers and cook in the oven for 6 to 7 minutes each side, basting occasionally with the marinade until cooked through.

4 portions

Chicken *is an excellent source of lean protein and is very versatile. It might be a good idea in this recipe to make skewers using chicken breast and chicken thigh together as the dark meat of the chicken contains twice as much iron and zinc as the light meat.*

Red meat *contains iron that is more easily absorbed than iron in fruit, vegetables, grains and eggs. However, meat will help to boost the absorption of iron from vegetables and cereals when eaten at the same time.*

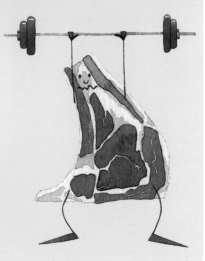

Meatballs with sweet and sour sauce and Chinese fried rice

These miniature meatballs are made with lean beef in a very tasty, tomato-flavoured sweet and sour sauce and served with Chinese fried rice (see page 123). This is a great favourite with all my family.

MEATBALLS

450 g (1 lb) lean minced beef

1 onion, peeled and finely chopped

1 apple, peeled and grated

50g (2 oz) fresh white breadcrumbs

1 tbsp chopped fresh parsley

1 chicken stock cube, finely crumbled

2 tbsp cold water

salt and freshly ground black pepper

2 tbsp vegetable oil

SWEET AND SOUR SAUCE

1 tbsp soy sauce

1/2 tbsp cornflour

1 tbsp vegetable oil

1 onion, peeled and finely chopped

**50 g (2 oz) red pepper (capsicum),
   de-seeded and diced**

1 x 400 g (14 oz) can chopped tomatoes

1 tbsp malt vinegar

1 tsp brown sugar

freshly ground black pepper

Mix together all the ingredients for the meatballs and chop for a few seconds in a food processor. Using floured hands, form into about 20 meatballs. Heat the oil in a frying pan and sauté the meatballs, turning occasionally, until browned and sealed (10 to 12 minutes).

Meanwhile, to make the sauce, mix together the soy sauce and cornflour in a small bowl. Heat the oil in a pan and sauté the onion for 3 minutes. Add the red pepper and sauté, stirring occasionally, for 2 minutes. Add the tomatoes, vinegar and sugar, season with pepper and simmer for 10 minutes. Add the soy sauce mixture and cook for 2 minutes, stirring occasionally. Blend and sieve or purée the sauce through a mouli. Pour the sauce over the meatballs, cover and simmer until cooked through (about 5 minutes).

SUPERFOODS

Red meat *is best included in your diet two or three times a week as it is the best source of readily absorbed iron. Iron requirements rise when the body is growing fast; so it is especially important to make sure your child gets enough iron between six months and two years.*

SUPERFOODS

Herbs *have many medicinal properties. Parsley contains vitamin C and iron and chewing on parsley is a good breath freshener, especially after eating garlic. Chewing thyme is thought to help soothe sore throats and oregano as an infusion is thought to aid digestion and relieve cold symptoms.*

Scarlett's spaghetti Bolognese

My daughter Scarlett, who is now nine years old, loves this recipes. Like so many children she would be happy to eat pasta every day. If your child prefers, leave out the mushrooms.

1 tbsp vegetable oil

1 onion, peeled and chopped

1 clove garlic, crushed

1 large carrot, grated

500 g (1 lb 2 oz) minced meat

125 g (4½ oz) button mushrooms, sliced

6 tbsp tomato purée (paste)

1 tsp mixed dried herbs

1 x 400 g (14 oz) can chopped tomatoes

150 ml (5 fl oz) chicken or beef stock

salt and freshly ground black pepper

200 g (7 oz) spaghetti

Heat the oil in a large saucepan or frying pan and sauté the onion and garlic for 3 minutes. Add the carrots and sauté for 2 minutes. Add the minced meat and sauté until browned all over, then add the mushrooms and fry for 2 minutes. Stir in the tomato purée and herbs and cook for 1 minute. Add the chopped tomatoes and stock and season with salt and pepper. Cover and cook for 15 minutes. Meanwhile, cook the spaghetti according to the packet instructions. When it's cooked, drain in a colander and toss with the Bolognese sauce.

Fillet of fish with herb butter

This would be good served with creamy mashed potatoes and peas.

25 g (1 oz) softened butter

2 tbsp chopped mixed fresh herbs,
  e.g. parsley, thyme, oregano, basil

1 tbsp fresh squeezed lemon juice

450 g (1 lb) thick fillets of cod, skinned

coarse sea salt and freshly ground
  black pepper

Pre-heat an oven to 180°C/350°F/Gas Mark 4. Mix the softened butter together with the chopped herbs and lemon juice. Place the fish in a small ovenproof dish, season with salt and pepper and then spread the herb butter over the top.

Place in the oven and cook until the fish is cooked through (8 to 10 minutes). Flake with a fork, checking to make sure that there are no bones.

Mini-fish pie

If you want your child to grow up liking fish then you have to try this super delicious mini-fish pie. If you make them in ramekin dishes they will be just the right size for your child to enjoy without feeling that there is just too much on the plate. It is good to keep a stock of these mini-fish pies in the freezer for days when you don't want to cook.

550 g (1 lb 4 oz) potatoes, peeled and diced

40 g (1½ oz) butter

4 tbsp milk

salt and freshly ground black pepper

1 small onion, finely chopped

2 tomatoes, skinned, de-seeded and chopped

40 g (1½ oz) butter

1½ tbsp flour

200 g (7 oz) cod fillets, skinned and cut into 2 cm (¾ inch) cubes

200 g (7 oz) salmon fillets, skinned and cut into 2 cm (¾ inch) cubes

1 tbsp chopped parsley (optional)

1 bay leaf

200 ml (7 fl oz) milk to cover

50 g (2 oz) Cheddar cheese, grated

1 lightly beaten egg

Cook the potatoes in a pan of lightly salted water until tender (about 15 minutes), then drain and mash together with the milk and butter and season to taste.

Melt the butter in a heavy based saucepan and sauté the onion for one minute. Add the chopped tomatoes and sauté for 2 to 3 minutes. Stir in the flour and cook for one minute. Add the milk, bring to the boil and cook for one minute. Stir in the cod, salmon, parsley (if using) and bay leaf and simmer for 3 to 4 minutes. Remove the bay leaf, stir in the grated Cheddar until melted and season to taste.

Pre-heat an oven to 180°C/350°F/Gas Mark 4. Divide the fish between four ramekin dishes about 8–10 cm (3–4 inches) in diameter and top with the mashed potato. Brush the potato with lightly beaten egg and cook in the oven for 15 to 20 minutes. You can brown under a pre-heated grill at the end if you wish.

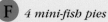 **F** *4 mini-fish pies*

White fish *such as cod is an excellent source of low-fat protein and contains selenium, calcium and magnesium. Eating fish helps fight free radicals and also boosts the immune system.*

SUPERFOODS

F *6 rissoles*

SUPERFOODS

Salmon *provides a good source of essential fats that support brain function and the immune system. Indeed, it is thought that the essential fatty acids in oily fish may help children who suffer from dyslexia or dyspraxia. An oily fish such as salmon should be included in all of our diets at least once a week.*

F *6 portions*

SUPERFOODS

Rice *contains starch that is digested and absorbed slowly, which provides a steady blood sugar level for long-lasting energy.*

Easy salmon rissoles

These salmon rissoles are really delicious and can be prepared in 10 minutes using store cupboard ingredients. They make good finger food and can also be eaten cold.

1 x 215 g (7½ oz) can red salmon
1 heaped tbsp grated or finely chopped onion
2 tbsp tomato ketchup
1 tbsp fine matzo meal or fresh breadcrumbs plus 25 g (1 oz) for coating
2 tbsp vegetable oil

Flake the salmon, checking carefully there are no bones. In a mixing bowl, combine the salmon, grated onion, ketchup and the 1 tablespoon of matzo meal or breadcrumbs. Form into six small rissoles and coat in matzo meal or breadcrumbs. Heat the oil in a frying pan and sauté the rissoles until golden (1 to 2 minutes each side).

Rice 'n' easy

A delicious, easy-to-prepare dish of cooked rice and tender pieces of chicken in a tasty tomato sauce. Rice tends to be very popular with young children and these are good textures to encourage your child to chew.

200 g (7 oz) long grain white rice
1 large shallot or 1 small onion, peeled and chopped
½ small red pepper (capsicum), de-seeded and chopped
1 tbsp chopped parsley
225 g (8 oz) chicken breast, chopped

450 ml (16 fl oz) passata (tomato purée)
1 chicken stock cube dissolved in 100 ml (3 fl oz) boiling water
1 tbsp garlic purée (paste)
1 tsp caster sugar
salt and freshly ground black pepper

Cook the rice according to the packet instructions. While the rice is cooking, heat the oil in a large saucepan and sauté the shallot, red pepper and parsley for about 5 minutes. Add the chopped chicken and sauté, stirring occasionally, until it turns opaque. Add the passata, the chicken stock, garlic purée and sugar and season with salt and pepper. Cook, uncovered, for 15 minutes. Drain the rice when cooked and mix with the tomato sauce.

Oven-baked root vegetable chips

These make a great-tasting finger food. You can also use other root vegetables like pumpkin or carrot. They are very good served with a little pot of sour cream and chive dip. For babies under a year, leave out the salt and seasoning.

100 g (4 oz) potatoes, scrubbed
100 g (4 oz) sweet potatoes, scrubbed
100 g (4 oz) parsnips, scrubbed
Schwartz Season-All Seasoning (Master Foods All Purpose Spicy Seasoning)
fresh ground sea-salt
1 tbsp olive oil

DIP
100 g (4 oz) cream cheese
½ tbsp tomato ketchup
½ tbsp full-fat milk
1 tsp snipped chives

Pre-heat an oven to 200°C/400°F/Gas Mark 6. Cut the potatoes and sweet potatoes in half lengthways and then into wedges. Cut the parsnips into wedges lengthways. Put all the pieces into a bowl and toss with the olive oil, a sprinkling of seasoning and a little salt (for babies over a year). Brush a roasting tin with a little olive oil and arrange the vegetable wedges in the tin. Bake in the oven until tender (about 30 minutes).

For the dip, mix together the cream cheese, ketchup and milk and stir in the snipped chives. Serve with the vegetable chips.

4 portions

Sweet potato *is high in vitamins A and C and is a particularly rich source of phytochemicals, which can help protect against disease.*

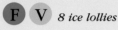

Fun ways with fruit

It is fun to arrange fruit in novelty shapes and only takes a few minutes – and your child will probably want to give you a helping hand. Here, the fish is made from kiwi, orange, mango, nectarine and grapes. Let your imaginations run free and set about creating your dream house, a car, a boat – whatever you or your children come up with. Different fruits contain different vitamins and minerals so the more variety the better.

Peach, strawberry and raspberry ice lollies (blocks)

If there is one food that almost no child can resist it has to be an ice lolly. Most of the lollies you buy are full of sugar, artificial colours and flavour but it takes very little time to make your own using good natural ingredients like puréed fresh fruit and fresh fruit juices.

200 g (7 oz) strawberries
150 g (5 oz) raspberries
50 g (2 oz) icing sugar, to taste
400 ml (14 fl oz) peach juice

Purée the strawberries and raspberries and push through a sieve. Stir in the icing sugar until dissolved. Mix the fruit purée with the peach juice and pour into ice-lolly (ice-block) moulds.

Lara's luscious lychee ice lollies (blocks)

1 x 425 g (15 oz) can lychees
1 tbsp freshly squeezed lemon juice

Blend the lychees together with the juice from the tin and sieve. Stir in the lemon juice and pour into ice-lolly (ice-block) moulds.

Summer fruit brûlée

150 g (5 oz) mixed berry fruits, fresh or frozen, e.g. strawberries, raspberries,
  blackberries, blueberries
150 ml (5 fl oz) double (thickened) cream
150 ml (5 fl oz) Greek yoghurt
2 tbsp icing sugar
vanilla essence
2 tbsp icing sugar for the topping

Divide the fruits between two small 10-cm (4-in) diameter ramekin dishes. Lightly whip the
double cream until it forms soft peaks. Fold in the Greek yoghurt, icing sugar and add a few
drops of vanilla essence.

Pre-heat the grill. Spoon the cream and yoghurt mixture over the fruits, smoothing over
the top. Sprinkle over the icing sugar, place the ramekins on a baking sheet and slide under
the hot grill. Grill until the sugar has caramelised.

V *2 fruit brûlées*

Blackberries *contain more vitamin E than any other fruit which is vital for the protection of the heart and arteries. They also contain vitamin C and iron.*

SUPERFOODS

Healthy eating:
Do not use low-fat or reduced-fat yoghurts, it is better to stick to full-fat natural yoghurts.

Peach melba smoothie

V *2 glasses*

There are times when children are off their food maybe because they are a little unwell or
maybe just because they are too busy playing to take the time to eat a proper meal. So
giving your child something nutritious to drink like a smoothie will ensure that she at least
gets some nutrients.

75 g (3 oz) raspberries
½ x 425 g (15 oz) can peaches in natural juice, drained
200 ml (7 fl oz) peach- or raspberry-flavoured drinking yoghurt
100 ml (3 fl oz) full-fat milk
1 tbsp icing sugar

Purée together the raspberries and peaches and push through a sieve to remove any seeds.
Using a hand blender, blend together the yoghurt, fruits, milk and icing sugar until smooth.

Yoghurt *provides a good source of calcium, protein and phosphorus, which are all important for strong healthy bones and teeth. Yoghurt is more easily digested than milk.*

SUPERFOODS

2 to 3 years:

SuperFoods for the growing years

Your child should now be enjoying a full and varied diet and you should be able to cook meals for the whole family to enjoy. Make sure you offer plenty of healthy snacks as many toddlers prefer lots of small meals to three big ones.

Healthy snacks

Young children require a large amount of energy in comparison to their body size but they cannot cope with large quantities of food at any one time. Some toddlers may survive quite happily on three meals a day but you will probably find that your child will also need snacks between meals to keep up her energy level. As babies become increasingly mobile and expend a lot of energy it is important that you have plenty of healthy snacks on hand rather than let her fill herself up on empty calories like sweet biscuits and potato crisps. Offer healthy snacks like cheese, dried or fresh fruit or sandwiches with nutritious fillings like peanut butter, Marmite or Promite.

Young children have to eat concentrated sources of energy and nutrients frequently. It's a good idea to keep a stock of foods that lend themselves to snacks but which are wholesome and will give a child a slow release of energy. This is preferable to a faster boost of energy followed by a more rapid drop in blood sugars as happens when sugary snacks are eaten.

Offer your child nutritious snacks like fruit or raw vegetables with a dip. It is regular snacking on sugary foods and drinks that does the most damage to children's teeth, so it is important to train young children to enjoy eating healthy snacks like the ones listed to the right.

You can aim towards a pattern of three meals a day but it will probably take a few years for toddlers to get there. Toddlers

Healthy eating: *Try to allow snacks only if more than an hour before the next meal so that children will still be hungry at mealtimes. Also try to restrict a snack to at least an hour after the last meal so that children don't get the idea that they can refuse a meal and then get something else to eat shortly afterwards.*

Healthy eating: *Potato crisps and corn snacks are all right as part of a balanced diet, but choose a variety made with natural ingredients (vegetable crisps are good) and preferably low-salt. Limit your child to three bags a week. Homemade popcorn is lower in fat and higher in fibre than potato crisps and similar snacks.*

only have small tummies and often can't eat enough at one meal to be sustained through to the next. Be prepared to offer your toddler healthy between-meal snacks during the day. So many of us will die from diet-related diseases that setting up a good diet in the vital first few years may well determine your child's health later in life.

Some ideas for healthy snacks

- Fresh fruit.
- Mini-sandwiches.
- Yoghurt or fromage frais.
- Wholegrain breakfast cereals.
- Steamed or raw vegetable sticks.
- Fingers of toast with Marmite or Promite.
- Pitta bread fingers and hummus.
- Rice cakes, sesame seed crackers, crispbread.
- Muffins.
- Crumpets or pikelets.
- Dried fruits.
- Cheese.
- Cream cheese with mini-bread sticks.
- A bowl of home-made soup or fresh soup from a carton.

Energy-rich snacks

Toddlers are usually very active and apart from mealtimes will need good healthy snacks to keep up their energy. Toddlers tend to need frequent small meals. Unrefined carbohydrate foods like wholemeal bread, wholegrain cereal or potatoes take longer to break down into glucose and will provide a more nutritious and sustained energy supply than sugar and carbohydrates from refined sources like white bread or chocolate biscuits. Fresh fruit also provides a good fast-working supply of energy.

Healthy junk food

There is no such thing as junk food only a junk diet! Hamburgers, chips, potato crisps and chocolate eaten in moderation provide energy, protein and even minerals like calcium. But it is now clear that a junk diet that is high in fat, sugar and salt leads to health problems like obesity, heart disease and cancer later on in life. Bad habits start very early on in life, so setting a good example by eating healthy foods will help protect your child's future.

Good foods for a quick spurt of energy
- Bowl of cornflakes.
- Banana.
- Raisins.
- Yoghurt and honey.

Good food for sustained energy
- Peanut butter sandwich on wholegrain bread.
- Baked beans on toast.
- Jacket potato with cheese.
- Bread with ham, tuna or cheese.
- Fresh fruit milkshake.

Of course, foods that are fried are not bad for children as fat is used by them as energy to grow and isn't related to any increased heart problems. But vegetable oils are better than animal fats. However, fried foods must only be used as part of a healthy diet because, like anything else, too great an amount of fried food can be bad for children.

Foods like burgers and pizzas tend to be very appealing and children may well resent not being allowed them, particularly if their friends get to eat them. However, a good solution is to prepare foods that look like the foods they want but are actually made from good healthy ingredients. Try Rabbit muffins (p94), Oven-baked root vegetable chips (p107) and Delicious chicken burgers (with four different vegetables) (p128).

Obesity in children

Shocking new figures show that 25% of children in England are overweight. One in six 10-year-olds are obese, and almost one in five 15-year-olds. Overweight children are more at risk of heart disease and diabetes. However, it is no surprise when today's children not only eat more but are becoming less and less active. Any parent who has tried to prise a child off the sofa or away from their computer to go outside and get some exercise will know that children are becoming increasingly sedentary, more often than not moving nothing but a few fingers on the television or video remote control. In a recent survey, 40 per cent of boys and 60 per cent of girls failed to meet the recommended minimum of 1 hour a day of moderate exercise.

Today's children are likely to live shorter lives than their parents. Lack of exercise and junk food diets mean that children are storing up serious health difficulties for the future – obesity, heart disease, weakened bone structure and cancer. When bones are forming, exercise is essential because it stimulates the deposition of minerals, especially calcium, in children's bones. If children are active, they will grow up with a good bone density, which reduces the risk of osteoporosis (weakened bones) later in life.

Chicken salad with sweetcorn, pasta and cherry tomatoes

600 ml (20 fl oz) chicken stock

2 small chicken breasts, cut into bite-sized pieces

100 g (4 oz) pasta shapes, cooked and cooled

100 g (4 oz) canned or cooked frozen sweetcorn

18 small cherry tomatoes, cut in half

2 spring onions, finely sliced

½ baby gem (cos) lettuce, shredded

DRESSING

3 tbsp olive oil

1 tbsp white wine vinegar

½ tsp Dijon mustard

½ tsp sugar

salt and pepper

1 tbsp from the chicken stock used to poach the chicken

Poach the chicken for 10 minutes and leave to cool completely. Then remove the chicken with a slotted spoon and cut into bite-sized pieces. This can be prepared the night before. To make the dressing, whisk together all of the ingredients (or use a hand blender). Mix together all of the salad ingredients and toss in the dressing.

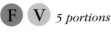
Special tomato pasta sauce

2 red peppers (capsicums), cored, de-seeded and cut into wide strips

1 shallot, peeled and finely chopped

1 small garlic clove, peeled and crushed

1 tbsp olive oil

350 g (12 oz) tomatoes, skinned, de-seeded and roughly chopped

250 ml (8 fl oz) vegetable stock

15 g (½ oz) butter

salt and freshly ground black pepper

Roast the red peppers under a pre-heated grill until the skin is charred on all sides. Place the peppers in a plastic bag and seal. Set aside to cool down a little. Meanwhile, sauté the shallots and garlic in the olive oil until softened but not coloured. Add the tomatoes and cook for 5 minutes. Remove the skin from the roasted peppers (this should come away easily) and add to the sauce together with the vegetable stock. Cook and put over a gentle heat for about 10 minutes. Stir in the butter, purée in a food processor and season to taste. Serve as a sauce for cooked pasta. The sauce is also very good served with chicken.

Crispy cheese, cabbage and potato bake

This tasty, thinly sliced potato gratin makes a delicious meal on a cold day together with something like a bowl of soup. It would also make a delicious accompaniment to a family meal.

25 g (1 oz) butter
1 large or 2 medium onions, peeled and very thinly sliced
150 ml (5 fl oz) single cream
675 g (1½ lb) potatoes, peeled and thinly sliced
200 g (7 oz) shredded green cabbage
salt and freshly ground black pepper
75 g (3 oz) Cheddar cheese
75 g (3 oz) grated Gruyère cheese
300 ml (10 fl oz) full-fat milk

Pre-heat an oven to 180°C/350°F/Gas Mark 4. Melt the butter in a saucepan over a low heat and cook the onion until softened. Cover the base of an 18 x 28 cm (7 x 11 in) baking dish with a thin layer of cream, then with a layer of potatoes and cabbage sprinkled with salt and pepper and spoon one-third of the onions on top. Mix together the cheeses and sprinkle one-third of the mixture over the onions.

Continue with two more layers of potato, cabbage, onions and cheese. Mix the milk together with the remaining cream and pour over the potato mixture. Bake uncovered for about 30 minutes, then cover with foil and bake for about 30 minutes more, until golden and crispy on top. Test with a knife to make sure the potatoes are soft.

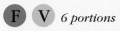 *6 portions*

Green cabbage *is rich in betacarotene and vitamin C. Cabbage belongs to the crucifer family whose protective powers against cancer have been demonstrated in many studies. The phytochemicals in cabbage were once thought to be poisonous to humans. It also contains antioxidants that fight coronary heart disease by mopping up free radicals.*

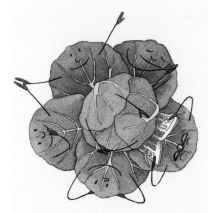

4 portions

Monounsaturated oils *such as olive oil can help to lower blood cholesterol levels. Interestingly, there is a lower incidence of cancer in Mediterranean countries where they use lots of olive oil. Olive oil is also a good source of vitamin E. Extra-virgin olive oil contains the highest quantity of protective antioxidants and has the best flavour.*

SUPERFOODS

Marinated chicken and vegetables on a griddle

Cooking food on a griddle is a very healthy way of cooking as it uses very little fat. Marinating the chicken before cooking it gives it a wonderful flavour and makes it nice and tender. Make sure the griddle is very hot before you lay the food on to it.

150 g (5 oz) new potatoes, cut in half

75 g (3 oz) broccoli florets

½ red pepper (capsicum), de-seeded and cut into strips

MARINADE

1 clove garlic, crushed

2 to 3 tbsp lemon juice

¼ tsp lemon zest

1 tsp caster sugar

1 tsp fresh oregano

2 chicken breasts

1 courgette (zucchini)

1 red onion

3 tbsp olive oil

Parboil the potatoes for about 10 minutes. Blanch the broccoli and red pepper for 1 minute. Thinly slice the chicken breasts into about six pieces each. Wash and cut the courgette into 12 mm (½ in) slices and peel and cut the onion into six to eight wedges.

For the marinade, mix together the garlic, lemon juice and zest, caster sugar and oregano. Stir the chicken into the marinade together with the prepared vegetables and leave to marinate for about 30 minutes.

Heat the griddle (or you can use a frying pan), brush with a little olive oil and remove the chicken from the marinade and cook for about 3 minutes on each side or until cooked through. Remove and keep warm. Repeat the same process with the vegetables, cooking in batches if necessary. Mix the chicken and vegetables together and serve.

SUPERFOODS

Garlic *has the reputation of a cure-all in folk medicine and has been proven to help develop resistance to infection. Garlic contains allicin, which acts as a natural antibiotic and antifungal, and it is also high in antioxidants. Worshipped by the Ancient Egyptians, chewed by Greek athletes and essential for keeping vampires at bay, garlic is also good for zapping bacteria, maintaining a healthy heart and warding off colds.*

F *4 portions*

SUPERFOODS

Mascarpone *is an Italian cream cheese that is high in energy and rich in both calcium and vitamin D, both of which are important for building and maintaining strong bones and teeth.*

Stir-fried noodles with chicken and beansprouts

2 chicken breasts

MARINADE
3 tbsp oyster sauce
1 tbsp soy sauce
1 tbsp lemon juice
1 tbsp brown sugar
1 clove garlic, crushed
¼ tsp grated ginger

150 g (5 oz) fine egg noodles
1½ tbsp oil
½ red pepper (capsicum), de-seeded and sliced into thin strips
4 spring onions, cut into 2 cm (¾ in) pieces
100 g (4 oz) beansprouts

Cut the chicken into strips, mix together all the ingredients for the marinade and marinate the chicken for between 30 minutes and 1 hour.

Cook the noodles in boiling water according to the packet instructions. Heat the oil in a wok, remove the chicken from the marinade and stir-fry in the oil with the red pepper for 2 minutes. Add the onion and beansprouts and stir-fry for 1 minute. Stir in the remaining marinade and simmer until heated through (1 to 2 minutes).

Penne with chicken in a creamy mushroom and cheese sauce

Since pasta is generally so popular with children, a good way to get them to eat other nutritious foods is to combine them with pasta.

125 g (4½ oz) penne
1 tbsp olive oil
150 g (5 oz) button mushrooms, sliced
1 clove garlic, crushed
1 large chicken breast, cut into strips (approx. 150 g/5 oz)

150 g (5 oz) mascarpone (Italian cream cheese)
50 g (2 oz) Gruyère cheese, grated
75 ml (2½ fl oz) chicken stock
1 tbsp fresh chopped oregano
salt and freshly ground black pepper

Cook the penne in a large pan of lightly salted water according to the packet instructions. Heat the olive oil and sauté the mushrooms and garlic for 3 minutes. Add the chicken and cook for a further 4 minutes. Stir in the mascarpone and Gruyère cheeses, stock and oregano and simmer until the cheese has melted and the sauce has thickened slightly (about 3 minutes). Season to taste and stir in the penne.

Chinese fried rice

 4 portions

This tends to be very popular with children and makes a good accompaniment to the sweet and sour chicken balls.

225 g (8 oz) basmati rice
75 g (3 oz) carrots, peeled and sliced
75 g (3 oz) frozen peas
75 g (3 oz) red pepper (capsicum), de-seeded and diced
2 eggs, lightly beaten
salt
3 tbsp vegetable oil
1 small onion, peeled and finely chopped
1 spring onion, finely sliced
1-2 tbsp soy sauce

Wash the rice thoroughly and cook according to the packet instructions in a saucepan of lightly salted water. Steam the carrots, peas and pepper until tender (about 5 minutes). Season the eggs with a little salt and fry them in a frying pan with 1 tablespoon of the oil until set as a thin omelette. Roll up into a sausage shape and cut into thin strips. Meanwhile, put 2 tablespoons of oil into a wok or frying pan and sauté the chopped onion until softened. Add the steamed vegetables and rice and cook, stirring, for 2 to 3 minutes. Add the egg and spring onion and cook, stirring, for 2 minutes more. Sprinkle with soy sauce before serving.

Brown rice *tends not to be used for Chinese fried rice, but it is an excellent source of energy. It's a good idea to get your child used to eating brown rice as it contains more minerals, vitamins and fibre than white rice and is therefore much more nutritious.*

SUPERFOODS

Spinach and ricotta cannelloni

This spinach filling is easy and quick to prepare and there are some good-quality, ready-prepared tomato sauces available that can be used to cover the cannelloni if you haven't the time to prepare your own home-made sauce.

**225 g (8 oz) frozen spinach
  or 450 g (1 lb) fresh**
15 g (½ oz) butter
100 g (4 oz) ricotta cheese
25 g (1 oz) Parmesan cheese, grated
40 g (1½ oz) mozzarella cheese, grated
pinch grated nutmeg
salt and freshly ground black pepper
8 no pre-cook cannelloni
TOMATO SAUCE
1 onion, peeled and finely chopped
1 clove garlic, crushed
1 bay leaf
1 tbsp olive oil

**500 ml (17 fl oz) passata
  (tomato purée)**
½ tsp sugar
salt and freshly ground black pepper

25 g (1 oz) Cheddar cheese, sliced

DECORATION
8 sautéed button mushrooms
20 stoned black olives
75 g (3 oz) fine egg noodles
1 carrot, peeled
**¼ red and green pepper (capsicum),
  de-seeded**

Pre-heat an oven to 180ºC/350ºF/Gas Mark 4. To make the tomato sauce, sauté the onion, garlic and bay leaf in the olive oil for 2 minutes. Add the passata and sugar, season to taste and simmer uncovered for about 8 minutes or until thickened. Remove the bay leaf from the tomato sauce.

Cook the spinach according to the packet instructions. Drain well and press out any excess liquid with a wooden spoon, then roughly chop the spinach. Melt the butter in a saucepan and sauté the spinach for 1 to 2 minutes. Add the ricotta, Parmesan and mozzarella cheeses and season to taste. Use this mixture to fill the cannelloni and arrange these in a single layer in a suitable ovenproof dish, leaving enough room for the mushroom faces and feet (see photograph). Cover with the tomato sauce. Bake in the oven for 25 to 30 minutes. Arrange the cheese slices over the tomato sauce to form a turned-down sheet and heat in the oven until melted.

To decorate, arrange the mushrooms as faces and add tiny triangles of black olive for eyes, fine egg noodles for hair with red and green pepper bows, carrot triangles for hats, and tiny strips of red pepper for the mouths. Finally, arrange the black olives as feet.

SUPERFOODS

Cheese *and dairy products contain calcium that can be absorbed by the body much more easily than calcium from other foods. Hard cheeses like Parmesan and Cheddar contain more calcium than soft cheeses like ricotta and cottage cheese. Eating cheese at the end of a meal can also help to fight tooth decay caused by sugary foods by reducing the acid levels in plaque, so the French tradition of finishing a meal with a little cheese is a good idea.*

Prawns *are rich in selenium and zinc, both of which are important to maintain a strong immune system. Zinc is also important for repair and healing. The noodles are a good source of carbohydrate for energy.*

Warning: *Shellfish are a common cause of food allergy - always make sure it is very fresh.*

Singapore stir-fried noodles

Offering foods from around the world will broaden your child's tastes and this dish should prove to be popular with the whole family. Too many children have a boring and repetitive diet of hamburgers, chips, pizza and other stereotyped 'children's foods'. There are now so many other choices available to us, especially with the greater variety of produce available in supermarkets like rice noodles, fresh ginger and Korma curry paste. Don't be afraid to make some more exotic dishes for your child: their tastes are often more sophisticated than we give them credit for.

150 g (5 oz) dried fine rice noodles or fine egg noodles

1 tbsp vegetable oil

½ clove garlic, crushed

¼ green chilli, finely diced

¼ tsp finely grated root ginger

1 small chicken breast, cut into very small pieces

50 g (2 oz) frozen peas

50 g (2 oz) cooked small prawns

2 spring onions, finely sliced

1 tbsp soy sauce

1 tbsp sake (rice wine)

pinch of sugar

2 tsp mild Korma curry paste

150 ml (5 fl oz) chicken stock

1 egg, lightly beaten

salt and white pepper

Place the noodles in a large bowl and cover with boiling water. Leave to stand for 3 minutes. If using Chinese noodles, follow the cooking instructions on the packet. Drain in a colander and then rinse thoroughly in cold water and leave to drain. Heat the oil in a wok and sauté the garlic, chilli and ginger for 1 minute. Add the chicken and stir-fry for 2 minutes. Add the peas, prawns and spring onion. Add the noodles and soy sauce, rice wine, sugar, curry paste and stock. Add the lightly beaten egg and cook, stirring, for 1 to 2 minutes. Season to taste.

Fish and chips in a comic

Serve these strips of fish with chips – and how about wrapping them in a comic instead of a newspaper for added child appeal? If you wish, you can line the comic with some greaseproof paper.

150 g (5 oz) skinned fillets of sole or plaice (lemon sole or flounder)
25 g (1 oz) flour
salt and freshly ground black pepper
cayenne pepper
1 egg, lightly beaten
125 g (4½ oz) dried breadcrumbs
sunflower oil for deep frying

TARTARE SAUCE
150 ml (5 fl oz) mayonnaise
lemon juice to taste
1 tbsp chopped parsley
1½ tbsp capers, chopped
2 tsp chopped gherkins
1 tbsp chopped chives

Cut the fish into strips and coat in flour seasoned with salt and pepper and cayenne pepper. Dip the coated fish into the egg and then coat the strips in the breadcrumbs and deep fry for 3 to 4 minutes in two batches.

To make the tartare sauce, simply mix together all the ingredients and serve with the fish and chips.

Fish *is a nutrient-dense source of protein and also a good source of vitamin B12. It is a good idea to include fish dishes regularly to allow children to get used to this very useful and healthy food in our diets.*

SUPERFOODS

Chewy oatmeal raisin cookies

These delicious cookies are quick and easy to make and very moreish. If you like you can add a little ground cinnamon to flavour them.

115 g (4½ oz) unsalted butter
100 g (4 oz) caster sugar
75 g (3 oz) soft brown sugar
1 egg
1 tsp pure vanilla essence

140 g (5 oz) plain flour
1 tsp baking powder
½ tsp salt
100 g (4 oz) rolled oats
100 g (4 oz) raisins

Pre-heat an oven to 180°C/350°F/Gas Mark 4. Beat the butter together with the sugars until light and fluffy. Beat in the egg and vanilla. Combine the flour, baking powder, salt and oats and stir these into the creamed butter and sugar mixture. Finally stir in the raisins.

Prepare two large greased or lined baking sheets. Form the mixture into walnut-sized balls and flatten them with your fingers onto the baking sheets. Space them well apart. Bake in the oven for about 15 minutes or until the edges are a light golden brown.

Traffic light ice lollies (blocks)

12 ice lollies

If there's one food that almost no child can resist it must surely be an ice lolly. Unfortunately most of the ice lollies that you buy in the shops are full of sugar, and artificial colourings and flavourings. If peaches are not in season you could use fresh orange juice instead. It's easy to make your own fruit lollies simply by pouring fresh fruit juice, like Cranberry and raspberry juice, or smoothies into ice-lolly moulds.

250 g (9 oz) strawberries
4½ tbsp runny honey

3 large ripe juicy peaches or nectarines, peeled, stoned and sliced
5 large ripe kiwi fruit, peeled and sliced

In a blender, purée the strawberries and then sieve the purée to get rid of the seeds. Stir 1½ tbsp of the honey into the strawberry purée. Then pour the strawberry purée into each of the ice-lolly moulds until each mould is one-third full and freeze until firm (about 1½ hours). Repeat this process with the peaches and 1½ tbsp of the honey (no need to sieve peaches), and then the kiwi fruit mixed with the rest of the honey.

3 years plus:
favourite family meals

To make food a fun and enjoyable experience for your child involve her in shopping and cooking. Encourage her to be adventurous and try some of the wonderful dishes from around the world in this chapter.

Ginger *aids digestion and is also a good remedy for nausea, particularly travel sickness. Grated fresh ginger in a hot lemon and honey drink can help alleviate the symptoms of a cold. Mix together the juice of half a lemon, some fresh grated ginger and a teaspoon or two of honey in a mug and top up with boiling water.*

Healthy eating:

If you don't want to make your own chicken stock, you can buy some good fresh liquid chicken stock in cartons in large supermarkets.

Chicken noodle soup

1 chicken breast

MARINADE
2 tbsp soy sauce
1 tsp sesame oil
½ tsp grated fresh ginger
1 tbsp honey
1 clove garlic, crushed

1.3 litres (2 pints) chicken stock
100 g (4 oz) egg noodles
75 g (3 oz) frozen or canned sweetcorn
3 spring onions, thinly sliced

Slice the chicken breast in half to make two thin fillets. Mix all the ingredients for the marinade and marinate the chicken for 30 minutes.

Bring the stock to the boil, then reduce the heat and poach the chicken for about 8 minutes. Remove the chicken with a slotted spoon, reserving the marinade, and allow to cool down slightly. Then shred the chicken very finely.

Cook the noodles according to the packet instructions. Stir the sweetcorn, spring onions and reserved marinade into the stock. Bring to the boil, then add the shredded chicken and noodles and heat through.

Nasi goreng

200 g (7 oz) long grain rice
4 shallots, cut into very fine rings (or use 2 small onions, peeled and sliced)
approximately 250 ml (8 fl oz) vegetable oil

OMELETTE
1 egg
salt
¼ tsp caster sugar
½ tsp water

STIR-FRY
1 chicken breast, cut into small strips
1 clove garlic, crushed
a pinch of mild chilli powder
100 g (4 oz) cooked prawns
4 spring onions, sliced
2 tbsp soy sauce
1 tbsp fresh chopped parsley

Cook the rice according to the packet instructions and leave to cool. Heat 2.5 cm (1 in) of oil in a small frying pan. To test if it is hot enough, drop a piece of shallot into the oil and if it sizzles and bubbles the oil is ready. Sauté the fine rings of shallot in two batches until golden brown (1 to 2 minutes) and drain these on kitchen paper.

To make the omelette, beat together the egg, salt, caster sugar and water. Heat 1 teaspoon of vegetable oil in a frying pan. Pour in the egg and swirl to thinly cover the base of the pan. Cook for about 1 minute until set, then turn over and cook for 30 seconds on the other side. Remove from the pan and cut into strips.

Heat 2 tablespoons of vegetable oil in a wok or frying pan and stir-fry the chicken and garlic for 3 to 4 minutes. Stir in the chilli powder, prawns and spring onions and stir-fry for about 2 minutes. Add the rice and stir in the soy sauce and chopped parsley and stir-fry for 4 to 5 minutes. Finally, stir in the strips of egg and golden shallots.

F *6 portions*

Prawns *are an excellent source of vitamin B12, which is necessary for the formation of blood cells and nerves, and also provide selenium, which is important for growth and helps protect against heart disease and cancer.*

SUPERFOODS

Thai-style chicken curry

4 portions

1 tbsp vegetable oil

2 large chicken breasts (approximately 300 g/10 oz)

150 g (5 oz) new potatoes, thinly sliced

1 x 400 ml (14 fl oz) can coconut cream

2 tsp green Thai curry paste

600 ml (1 pint) chicken stock

75 g (3 oz) French beans, trimmed

75 g (3 oz) baby corn

100 g (4 oz) broccoli florets, chopped

12 cherry tomatoes, halved

1 tsp caster sugar

1 tsp lime or lemon juice

Heat the oil in a wok or large frying pan and fry the chicken and potatoes until the chicken turns opaque (3 to 4 minutes). Stir in the coconut cream, Thai curry paste and chicken stock. Bring to the simmer and cook for 5 to 6 minutes, then add the beans, baby corn and broccoli. Simmer until the vegetables are tender (a further 8 to 10 minutes). Stir in the cherry tomatoes, sugar and lime or lemon juice.

Healthy eating:
Many children's diets can be rather unadventurous, consisting of the usual burgers, pizzas and chicken nuggets. Introduce children to a wide variety of flavours so they don't grow up to be fussy eaters. Mild curry is often very popular, particularly when it is combined with coconut cream, as here.

Pilau rice

4 portions

This rice has a wonderful flavour and the turmeric turns the rice a rich yellow colour, which is very attractive.

200 g (7 oz) basmati rice

15 g (1/2 oz) butter

1/2 tsp turmeric

2 cardamom pods

2 cloves

1/2 cinnamon stick

350 ml (11 fl oz) boiling water

salt

Rinse the rice until the water runs clear through a sieve.

In a medium saucepan, melt the butter and stir in the rice and spices until evenly coated in butter. Stir in the boiling water and a pinch of salt. Cover and leave to cook on the lowest heat for 10 minutes. Remove from the heat and leave in the pan, without stirring, for 10 minutes. Remove the cardamom, cinnamon stick and cloves, and fluff up with a fork.

Spices *have specific health benefits. It is believed that cardamom, for example, can relieve indigestion and can be used to aid coughs and colds. Cinnamon can help indigestion, diarrhoea and relieve nasal congestion and turmeric can help calm inflammation and relieve indigestion.*

SUPERFOODS

SUPERFOODS

Tomato ketchup

requires 25 tomatoes to fill one bottle. Lycopene, the natural red pigment found in tomatoes, has been linked with a lower risk of prostate cancer and heart disease. For years, nutritionists have emphasised the benefits of fresh fruits and vegetables. However, lycopene is easier for our bodies to absorb when the tomatoes have been cooked or processed with a little oil into foods such as ketchup or pasta sauce.

Chicken cannelloni

Decorating this tasty cannelloni to look like people sleeping in a bed will add oodles of child appeal (see Spinach and ricotta cannelloni on page 127). Older children will love to help.

CHICKEN AND TOMATO FILLING

1 onion, peeled and chopped

1 small clove garlic, crushed

1 tbsp olive oil

40 g (1½ oz) mushrooms, chopped

½ tsp dried herbs (Dried Mixed Herbs)

225 g (8 oz) minced chicken

½ x 400 g (14 oz) can chopped tomatoes

½ tbsp tomato ketchup

CHEESE SAUCE

25 g (1 oz) butter

25 g (1 oz) flour

½ tsp paprika

400 ml (14 fl oz) full-fat milk

100 g (4 oz) Cheddar cheese, grated

8 no pre-cook cannelloni

Sauté the onion and garlic for 2 minutes in the oil. Then add the mushrooms, herbs and chicken and sauté for 3 minutes. Stir in the chopped tomatoes and ketchup and simmer for 20 minutes.

To make the cheese sauce, melt the butter and stir in the flour and paprika and cook for 1 minute. Gradually whisk in the milk. Bring to the boil and then simmer, stirring, until thickened. Stir in 50 g (2 oz) of the grated Cheddar cheese.

Pre-heat an oven to 180°C/350°F/Gas Mark 4. Stuff the cannelloni with the chicken filling and arrange them in a shallow ovenproof dish. Pour over the cheese sauce and sprinkle with the remaining Cheddar cheese and bake in the oven for 25 minutes.

Mini-veal schnitzel with rösti

4 veal escalopes (approximately 275 g/9½ oz)

salt and freshly ground black pepper

1 tbsp lemon juice

flour for coating

1 egg, lightly beaten

seasoned breadcrumbs

vegetable oil for frying

ROSTI

1 small onion, peeled

500 g (1 lb 2 oz) potatoes, peeled

1 clove garlic, crushed

50 g (2 oz) butter

For the veal, place the escalopes between plastic wrap and flatten with a mallet until they are quite thin. Season with salt, pepper and lemon juice and then coat in flour. Dip in the egg and then into the seasoned breadcrumbs. Then sauté the escalopes in the vegetable oil for about 2 to 3 minutes on each side.

For the rösti, grate the onion and potatoes and then mix with the crushed garlic and season with salt and pepper. Take a small handful, squeeze out the excess liquid and sauté in the butter for 3 to 4 minutes on each side.

Marinated lamb cutlets

4 lamb cutlets

MARINADE

2 tsp lemon juice

1 tsp soy sauce

1 tsp sesame oil

1 tsp soft brown sugar

½ tsp herbes de Provence (Dried
    Mixed Herbs)

pinch of salt

freshly ground black pepper

Mix together all the ingredients for the marinade and marinate the lamb for at least 1 hour. Remove from the marinade and cook under a medium to high grill for about 8 minutes, turning halfway through and basting occasionally. Boil any remaining marinade and pour over the lamb cutlets.

4 portions

Veal *is a good source of protein, vitamin B12 and zinc and contains just under half the fat of lean red meat. This recipe could also successfully be made with chicken breasts.*

4 portions

Red meat and lamb *provide the best source of iron followed by pork and chicken. Lamb contains all the essential amino acid needed for growth and repair of tissue damage. Children grow so quickly they need regular high-protein foods. For young children, cut the lamb into small cubes and remove all the fat.*

SUPERFOODS

SUPERFOODS

SUPERFOODS

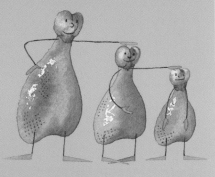

Delicious chicken fajitas

These are a great favourite of mine and I have made them much less hot and spicy so that children will enjoy eating them. My children love to assemble these and roll them up themselves. Everything can be prepared in advance.

2 small chicken breasts, cut into strips
¹⁄₈ tsp paprika
¹⁄₈ tsp mild chilli powder
¹⁄₈ tsp cumin (optional)
¹⁄₄ tsp oregano
1 tbsp plus 1 tsp olive oil
1 clove garlic, crushed
1 onion, peeled and thinly sliced
¹⁄₂ small red pepper (capsicum), de-seeded and thinly sliced

8 small flour tortillas
75 g (3 oz) shredded Iceberg lettuce
75 g (3 oz) Cheddar cheese, grated
3 tbsp sour cream

TOMATO SALSA
¹⁄₂ tbsp olive oil
¹⁄₄ green chilli, finely sliced
¹⁄₂ onion, peeled and chopped
¹⁄₄ small green pepper (capsicum), de-seeded and diced
1 small clove garlic
¹⁄₂ tsp red wine vinegar
1 x 200 g (7 oz) can chopped tomatoes
salt and freshly ground black pepper
¹⁄₂ tbsp parsley

Toss the chicken in the paprika, chilli powder, cumin and oregano. Heat 1 teaspoon of the oil in a pan and sauté the chicken, stirring occasionally, for 3 to 4 minutes. Remove the chicken with a slotted spoon. Add the remaining tablespoon of oil and sauté the garlic, onion and red pepper for 5 minutes. Return the chicken to the pan, season to taste and heat through.

To make the tomato salsa, heat the oil and fry the chilli, onion, pepper and garlic for about 5 minutes. Add the vinegar and cook for about 20 seconds. Add the chopped tomatoes, salt and pepper and parsley and simmer, uncovered, for about 15 minutes.

To assemble, heat the tortillas in the microwave according to the packet instructions. Then place some of the chicken mixture along the centre of each tortilla, top with some tomato salsa, shredded lettuce, grated cheese and a little sour cream and roll up.

Minced beef *is an excellent source of iron. A lack of iron will not only make your child feel tired but can also lower resistance to infection. Always choose lean cuts of meat. You may prefer to mince your own meat or ask your butcher to mince some good cuts for you.*

....

Warning: *Undercooked burgers may contain harmful bacteria such as E coli.*

 F *4 portions*

Red meat *is packed full of high quality protein as well as being the best source of easily absorbed iron. It is also a good source of zinc and vitamin B12.*

My favourite beefburgers

450 g (1 lb) minced beef, lamb or chicken
1 medium onion, peeled and finely chopped
½ red pepper (capsicum), cored, de-seeded and chopped
1 tbsp vegetable oil
2 tbsp finely chopped fresh parsley
½ chicken stock cube, dissolved in 3 tbsp boiling water
25 g (1 oz) breadcrumbs
1 Granny Smith apple, peeled and grated
salt and freshly ground black pepper
vegetable oil for frying

mini-rolls, sliced tomato, lettuce

BARBECUE SAUCE

2 tbsp vegetable oil
1 red onion, diced
1 clove garlic, crushed
200 ml (7 fl oz) passata (tomato purée)
2 tbsp tomato purée (paste)
½ tsp English mustard powder
2 tbsp white wine vinegar
2 tbsp dark brown sugar
1 tbsp Worcestershire sauce
a few drops Tabasco

Sauté the onion and red pepper until soft (about 5 minutes). Combine these with all the other ingredients and, using your hands, form into about six burgers. Shallow fry in vegetable oil until browned and cooked through (about 5 minutes each side). Alternatively, cook the burgers under a pre-heated grill or on a barbecue. For the sauce, heat the oil in a small pan and sauté the onion and garlic for 3 to 4 minutes until softened. Add the remaining ingredients for the sauce, cover with a lid and simmer for about 8 minutes. Purée in a hand blender to make a smooth sauce.

Stir-fried shredded beef

1 tbsp sesame oil
1 clove garlic, crushed
1 medium carrot, cut into matchsticks
1 small courgette (zucchini), cut into matchsticks
½ yellow pepper (capsicum), de-seeded and cut into matchsticks

300 g (10 oz) beef fillet, cut into very fine strips
1 tbsp cornflour
150 ml (5 fl oz) beef stock
2 tbsp dark brown sugar
2 tbsp soy sauce
a few drops Tabasco
1 tbsp sesame seeds

Heat the sesame oil in a wok and stir-fry the garlic, carrots, courgettes and pepper for 3 to 4 minutes. Add the beef and continue to stir-fry for 4 to 5 minutes. Mix the cornflour together with a tablespoon of water and stir into the beef stock. Stir this into the pan together with the sugar, soy sauce, Tabasco and sesame seeds. Bring to the simmer, cook until slightly thickened, and serve with rice.

Mild beef curry

F *6 portions*

Young children often have more sophisticated tastes than we give them credit for and it's important to introduce lots of variety at a young age when children are more likely to accept new tastes. Children will love curry when it is made like this. Serve with pilau rice (see page 161).

1 tbsp vegetable oil

2 onions, peeled and chopped

1 clove garlic, crushed

½ tsp grated fresh ginger

500 g (1 lb 2 oz) stewing steak (blade or round) or fillet steak cut into
  2.5 cm (1 in) cubes

2 tbsp mild curry powder

1 green pepper (capsicum), cored, de-seeded and cut into 2.5 cm (1 in) pieces

200 ml (8 fl oz) beef stock

2 tbsp tomato purée (paste)

200 ml (8 fl oz) double (thickened) cream

1 tbsp ground almonds

salt and freshly ground black pepper

3 tomatoes, skinned, de-seeded and chopped

Heat the oil in a large saucepan and fry the onion, garlic and ginger until softened (5 to 6 minutes). Stir in the beef and curry powder and cook until browned all over (2 to 3 minutes). Stir in the green pepper and cook for 1 minute. Stir in the beef stock, tomato purée, double cream and almonds and season with salt. Bring to the boil and simmer for 45 minutes, then stir in the tomatoes and cook until thickened (a further 10 to 15 minutes). Check seasonings.

Red meat *provides the best source of iron, which is important for healthy red blood cells. Children need increasing amounts of iron as they grow so rapidly. The brain is the largest store of iron and it is essential that adequate iron is present in the diet to support good brain development.*

SUPERFOODS

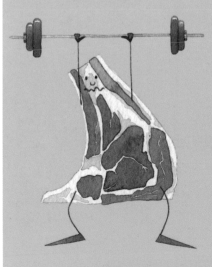

Tinned tuna *is a good source of vitamins, especially vitamins D and B12. It is also a good source of the anti-oxidant selenium, which helps to protect us against heart disease and cancer. Eating an oily fish like tuna once a week has been shown to reduce heart disease.*

Nuts *are great for vegetarians as they supply many of the nutrients usually found in animal sources. Combining cashew nuts with tofu, as in this recipe, makes for a good source of protein. Cashew nuts, like olive oil, are rich in heart-protecting monounsaturated fats.*

Tuna tortilla roll-ups

100 g (4 oz) tuna in oil
1 tbsp mayonnaise
½ tsp lemon juice
¼ tsp paprika
50 g (2 oz) frozen or canned sweetcorn

40 g (1½ oz) thinly sliced cucumber, red pepper (capsicum) or celery
shredded Iceberg lettuce
2 mini-tortillas
2 chives (optional)

Drain the tuna and mix together with the mayonnaise, lemon juice and paprika. Stir in the sweetcorn and cucumber, red pepper or celery. Place the tuna mixture along the centre of the tortilla. Cover with some shredded lettuce and roll up. You can then secure the tortilla by tying a chive around it.

Tofu and vegetable burgers

BURGERS
100 g (4 oz) broccoli florets
15 g (½ oz) butter
200 g (7 oz) button mushrooms, roughly chopped
1 clove garlic, crushed
1 x 285 g (9½ oz) packet firm tofu
100 g (4 oz) unsalted cashew nuts
3 spring onions, finely sliced

1 medium carrot, finely grated
100 g (4 oz) fresh breadcrumbs
1 tbsp oyster sauce
1 tbsp honey

salt and freshly ground black pepper
flour for coating
vegetable oil for frying

Blanch the broccoli in lightly salted boiling water until tender (about 2 minutes). Melt the butter in a frying pan and sauté the mushroom and garlic until softened (3 to 4 minutes). Transfer to a food processor with the broccoli and all of the other burger ingredients. Process until mixed together and season with salt and pepper.

Form into eight burgers, coat in flour and sauté over a medium heat until golden (2 to 3 minutes on each side).

Spinach, cheese and tomato lasagne

F V *5 portions*

TOMATO SAUCE

2 tbsp olive oil

1 large onion, peeled and chopped

1 kg (2 lb 4 oz) plum tomatoes, skinned,
de-seeded and chopped, or use two 400 g
cans chopped tomatoes

1 clove garlic, crushed

75 ml (2½ fl oz) vegetable stock

2 tbsp tomato purée (paste)

1 tsp caster sugar

1 bay leaf

1 tsp balsamic vinegar

6 basil leaves, roughly torn

salt and freshly ground black pepper

CHEESE SAUCE

40 g (1½ oz) butter

40 g (1½ oz) flour

400 ml (14 fl oz) milk

generous pinch ground nutmeg

40 g (1½ oz) grated Gruyère cheese

40 g (1½ oz) grated Cheddar cheese

salt and freshly ground black pepper

500 g (1 lb 2 oz) fresh baby spinach,
carefully washed, or use 250 g (9 oz)
frozen leaf spinach

9 sheets fresh or no pre-cook lasagne

3 tbsp grated Parmesan

Heat the oil in a large saucepan and sauté the onion for 2 to 3 minutes. Stir in the tomatoes and garlic, bring to the simmer and stir in the vegetable stock, tomato purée, caster sugar, bay leaf and balsamic vinegar. Cover and simmer for 20 minutes. Remove the lid and simmer to thicken the sauce for a further 10 minutes. Stir in the basil and season to taste.

To make the cheese sauce, melt the butter in a saucepan, stir in the flour and cook for one minute over a low heat. Gradually whisk in the milk and nutmeg, bring to the boil and then cook for one minute until thickened and smooth. Remove from the heat and stir in the grated Gruyère and Cheddar cheeses until melted. Season with salt and pepper.

Cook the spinach in a large pan with just a little water clinging to the leaves until wilted (about 3 minutes). Gently press out any excess liquid and roughly chop the spinach.

Pre-heat an oven to 180ºC/350ºF/Gas Mark 4. To assemble the lasagne, spread a little of the cheese sauce over the base of a lasagne dish measuring approximately 25 x 18 cm (10 x 7 in) and cover with three sheets of lasagne (break the third sheet into smaller pieces to fit the dish if necessary). Arrange half the spinach over the lasagne and top with one third of the cheese sauce and half the tomato sauce. Arrange another layer of lasagne on top and repeat with the spinach, cheese sauce and tomato sauce. Arrange another 3 sheets of lasagne on top and finally spread the remainder of the cheese sauce over the pasta to cover it completely. Sprinkle the top with the grated Parmesan cheese and cook in the oven for 30 minutes.

Finish off by browning the top under a pre-heated grill for a few minutes.

SUPERFOODS

Basil *can aid digestion, easing the symptoms of wind, stomach cramps, colic and indigestion.*

Healthy eating:

Fresh basil and tomato are perfect partners in this delicious lasagne, which makes a popular family meal. Always tear basil leaves rather than cut them to preserve their flavour.

V *12 burgers*

Onions and leeks

have a protective action on the circulatory system that helps to prevent your blood clotting. With children eating more and more junk food, fatty deposits in the arteries can now be found in even the youngest children.

Mini-vegetable burgers

Mushrooms, carrots, leek and onion all disappear into these burgers. It's good to make more than you need and freeze some for days when you don't want to cook.

1 potato (approx. 150 g/5 oz)

2 tbsp olive oil

1 small red onion, peeled and chopped

1 medium carrot, grated

¼ leek (approx. 45 g/2 oz), washed and finely chopped

50 g (2 oz) brown-cap mushrooms, chopped

1 clove garlic, crushed

½ tsp fresh thyme leaves

1 tbsp soy sauce

70 g (3 oz) Gruyère cheese, grated

½ tsp Worcestershire sauce

¾ tbsp honey

1 egg yolk

1 large pinch of cayenne pepper

salt and freshly ground black pepper

COATING

1 tbsp grated Parmesan

90 g (4 oz) fresh white breadcrumbs (approx. 2 slices of bread)

3 tbsp plain flour

1 egg, beaten

sunflower oil for frying

Boil the potato (unpeeled) in lightly salted water until tender (about 25 minutes). Drain and when cool enough to handle, peel and grate into a large bowl.

Meanwhile, heat the olive oil in a large non-stick frying pan. Sauté the onion for 3 minutes, then add the carrot, leek, mushrooms, garlic and thyme and sauté for 10 minutes. Cool slightly and then add to the potato.

Mix in the soy sauce, cheese, Worcestershire sauce, honey and egg yolk and season to taste with salt, pepper and the cayenne pepper.

Form into 12 small burgers. Mix the Parmesan with the breadcrumbs. Coat each burger with flour, dip into beaten egg and then dip in the breadcrumbs.

Heat some oil in a large frying pan. Sauté as many burgers as will comfortably fit in the pan, flipping at least once, until they are golden on both sides (about 2 minutes each side).

V *6 portions*

SUPERFOODS

Berry fruits *are rich in vitamin C, which is important for growth, healing of wounds and healthy skin.*

Mixed berry and peach crumble

Here is a truly delicious crumble made from mixed frozen berries and canned peaches. I put a layer of ground almonds into the crumble dish before I spoon in the summer berries to soak up some of the juices that are released from the fruit during cooking so that they do not bubble over the crumble topping and make it go soggy. Serve hot on its own or with ice cream or custard.

CRUMBLE TOPPING
125 g (4½ oz) plain flour
100 g (4 oz) rolled oats
75 g (3 oz) brown sugar
pinch of salt
125 g (4½ oz) butter

75 g (3 oz) ground almonds
1 x 400 g (14 oz) can of peaches
400 g (14 oz) fresh or frozen mixed berry fruits, e.g. raspberries, blackberries, strawberries, blueberries
100 g (4 oz) caster sugar

Pre-heat an oven to 200°C/400°F/Gas Mark 6. To make the topping, mix together the flour, oats, brown sugar and pinch of salt, cut the butter into pieces and rub in with your fingers until the mixture resembles coarse breadcrumbs. Spread the ground almonds over the base of a 20-cm (8-in) diameter round ovenproof dish. Mix the peaches and berry fruits together with the caster sugar and spoon into the dish. Sprinkle the crumble topping over the fruits and bake until golden (about 30 minutes).

Caramelised apple crumble

This is my favourite recipe for apple crumble and it is very easy to make. Serve hot with custard or vanilla ice-cream. If you like you could add some blackberries or blueberries to the apples once they are cooked.

750 g (1½ lb) cooking apples, peeled and diced
85 g (3½ oz) unsalted butter
75 g (3 oz) light muscovado sugar

CRUMBLE TOPPING
50 g (2 oz) ground almonds
50 g (2 oz) light muscovado sugar
100 g (4 oz) cold butter, diced
50 g (2 oz) porridge oats
1 tsp cinnamon
generous pinch of salt

Pre-heat an oven to 180°C/350°F/Gas Mark 4. Melt the butter and sugar until bubbling. Stir in the apples and cook over a medium to high heat for about 5 minutes.

In a large bowl, mix together all the ingredients for the topping and rub them together with your fingers to make the crumble.

Sprinkle a heaped tablespoon of ground almonds into the base of an 18 cm/7 in round ovenproof dish. Spoon the cooked apples on top and cover with the crumble topping. Sprinkle a little water over the topping and bake in the oven for 30 minutes.

Apples *An apple makes an ideal healthy snack – easy to carry, filling and refreshing. Some varieties are a good source of vitamin C which helps to maintain the immune system. Traditionally apples are used to treat digestive upsets. Uncooked apples are good for treating constipation, while stewed apples are good for diarrhoea and gastroentiritis.*

SUPERFOODS

Mixed berry and white chocolate cheesecake

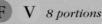

F V *8 portions*

BISCUIT BASE

250 g (9 oz) digestive (oatmeal) biscuits

125 g (4¹/₂ oz) butter, melted

CHEESECAKE

150 g (5 oz) white chocolate

1 tsp vanilla extract or 1 vanilla pod

225 ml (7 fl oz) double (thickened) cream

300 g (10 oz) Philadelphia cream cheese

TOPPING

**400 g (14 oz) mixed summer berries, e.g. strawberries, blackberries, raspberries,
  blueberries, redcurrants**

2 tbsp raspberry jam

2 tsp water

50 g (2 oz) white chocolate

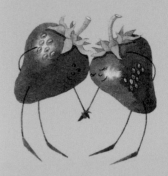

Summer berries *are packed with vitamin C, which helps to strengthen the immune system and fight infections. Vitamin C also aids the absorption of iron.*

SUPERFOODS

To make the base, crush the digestive biscuits by putting them in a plastic bag and crushing them with a rolling pin and then mix with the melted butter. Press them into the base of a lightly oiled 20-cm (8-in) diameter, loose-bottomed or spring-clip tin (this can be done with a potato masher). Place in the refrigerator to chill.

Melt the white chocolate in a heatproof bowl over a pan of simmering water. Add the vanilla extract to the cream or, if using a vanilla pod, split the pod with a sharp knife and scrape the seeds into the cream. Whip the cream until it forms fairly stiff peaks, and gently fold into the white chocolate mixture. Pour on top of the base and set aside in the refrigerator for at least 2 hours to set.

Once the cake is set, carefully remove from the tin. Arrange the berries on top of the cake. Heat the jam with the water and strain through a sieve. Leave to cool for about 1 minute and gently brush over the fruits. Melt the white chocolate and drizzle over the top of the fruits using a teaspoon.

F **V** *6 small ice lollies*

Strawberry sorbet ice lollies (blocks)

50 g (2 oz) caster sugar

60 ml (2 fl oz) water

250 g (9 oz) strawberries, hulled and cut in half

1 medium orange, squeezed

Put the sugar and water into a saucepan and boil until syrupy (about 3 minutes). Allow to cool. Purée the strawberries and sieve to get rid of the seeds. Combine the strawberry purée, syrup and orange juice and pour this mixture into ice-lolly (ice-block) moulds. Freeze until solid.

V *12 squares*

Did you know?

There is a good reason to crave chocolate, as eating chocolate makes us feel good since it triggers the release of serotonin and endorphin levels in the brain, which have an uplifting effect.

Dark and white chocolate refrigerator cake

200 g (7 oz) plain chocolate

75 g (3 oz) golden syrup

75 g (3 oz) unsalted butter

150 g (6 oz) digestive biscuits

75 g (3 oz) dried apricots, chopped

50 g (2 oz) raisins

50 g (2 oz) pecans, finely chopped

40 g (1½ oz) Rice Krispies

60 g (2½ oz) white chocolate, chopped into small pieces

Line a 23 cm (9 in) square shallow tin with clingfilm, leaving enough to hang over the sides of the tin.

Melt the plain chocolate, syrup and butter in a heatproof bowl set over a pan of simmering water, making sure the bottom of the bowl does not touch the water. Stir occasionally until melted, then set aside to cool down.

Break the digestive biscuits into small pieces, and mix together with the chopped apricots, raisins, pecans, Rice Krispies and chopped white chocolate. Stir these into the melted chocolate mixture. Spoon the mixture into the prepared tin and level the surface by pressing down gently with a potato masher or the back of a spoon. Place in the fridge to set, which should take 1 to 2 hours. To serve, carefully peel off the film and cut into 12 squares.

Cranberry, lemonade and orange juice ice lollies (blocks)

F V *4 ice lollies*

250 ml (8 fl oz) cranberry juice

100 ml (3 fl oz) lemonade

100 ml (3 fl oz) fresh orange juice

Mix together all the ingredients. Pour into ice-lolly (ice-block) moulds and freeze.

Cranberries *are rich in vitamin C: indeed, there is as much vitamin C in a glass of cranberry juice as there is in a glass of orange juice.*

Carrot cake with frosted icing

F V *10 portions*

225 ml (7½ fl oz) sunflower oil

150 g (5 oz) soft brown sugar

3 eggs

115 g (4½ oz) golden syrup

250 g (9 oz) self-raising flour

1 tsp bicarbonate of soda

1 tsp ground cinnamon

½ tsp ground ginger

½ tsp mixed spice

150 g (5 oz) grated carrot

40 g (1½ oz) desiccated coconut

FROSTED ICING

200 g (7 oz) full-fat cream cheese, e.g. Philadelphia

100 g (4 oz) icing sugar, sifted

1 vanilla pod or a few drops pure vanilla essence

Carrots *are rich in antioxidants, which are effective in supporting the body's immune system. One medium carrot will supply a six-year-old child's daily requirement of vitamin A.*

Pre-heat an oven to 150°C/300°F/Gas Mark 2. Whisk the oil, sugar, eggs and syrup until combined. Sieve in the flour, bicarbonate of soda and spices and then stir in the carrots and desiccated coconut. Pour into a 20-cm (8-in) square or round tin that has been greased and lined and bake in the oven for 40 to 45 minutes until cooked. Test to see that a skewer comes out clean. Remove from the oven and leave to cool in the tin for 10 minutes.

To make the icing, beat the cream cheese together with the icing sugar. Split the vanilla pod, scrape out the tiny black seeds using the point of a sharp knife and mix with the icing (if using essence, mix a few drops into the icing). Spread the icing over the top and sides of the cake when it is completely cool.

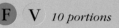

Tip

Leaf gelatine is amazing: it dissolves like a dream every time, unlike powdered gelatine which so often leaves stubborn little grains behind. You should be able to buy leaf gelatine in most large supermarkets.

Cranberry and raspberry jelly with summer fruits

This is a fantastic-looking dessert made with fresh fruit and fresh juice and it's very easy to prepare. You can either make one large jelly or individual jellies. If you can't find leaf gelatine, you could use two 10 g (¼ oz) sachets of powdered gelatine.

6 leaves gelatine

600 ml (1 pint) cranberry and raspberry juice

60 g (2½ oz) caster sugar

350 g (12 oz) mixed berries, e.g. blackberries, raspberries, blueberries, redcurrants and strawberries (when berry fruits are out of season you can use frozen berries)

RASPBERRY COULIS

200 g (8 oz) raspberries

2 tbsp icing sugar

To make the jelly, place the leaf gelatine in a shallow dish and pour over just enough cranberry and raspberry juice to cover the surface. Leave to soften for about 5 minutes.

Heat the remaining cranberry and raspberry juice and caster sugar in a saucepan until piping hot. Mix in the softened leaf gelatine and any juice, stirring until completely dissolved. Set aside to cool.

If using fresh fruit, halve the strawberries and remove the redcurrants from their stalks. Rinse a jelly mould (approx. 750 ml/1½ pint size) but do not dry (a wet mould will make it easier to remove the jelly when it is set). Spoon in the fruit, pour over 300 ml (10 fl oz) of the juice and leave in the fridge for about 1 hour or until beginning to set. When set, pour over the remaining juice to cover and return to the fridge to set. You could also pour the jelly into a loaf tin. Alternatively, divide the berries between 4 to 6 individual jelly moulds (or use glass dishes) and pour over the jelly. Leave in the fridge to set.

To make the coulis, blitz together the raspberries and icing sugar and push through a sieve to give a smooth sauce. Stir in any extra icing sugar if necessary.

To turn out the jelly, dip the mould into a bowl of hot water and run a knife around the edge of the mould or loaf tin to loosen the jelly. Invert onto a large plate and give it a quick shake and the jelly should slide out.

Serve the jelly with a little raspberry coulis and maybe some vanilla ice-cream.

Apple, oat and raisin muffins

V *10 muffins*

Oats *are high in soluble fibre, which helps lower blood cholesterol and also provides lasting energy, keeping hunger pangs at bay. Oat porridge is an ideal start to the day and should keep you full of energy.*

SUPERFOODS

These are known in my house as my one-legged muffins as I made them after returning from a skiing holiday when I broke my leg. Luckily my two daughters, Lara and Scarlett, were very willing helpers in the kitchen, gathering together ingredients and helping me experiment until we collectively came up with this very delicious muffin recipe, which is now a family favourite.

1 egg
150 ml (5 fl oz) sunflower oil
175 ml (6 fl oz) full-fat milk
75 g (3 oz) porridge oats
125 g (4½ oz) plain flour
3 tsp baking powder
75 g (3 oz) caster sugar
¾ tsp salt
½ tsp mixed spice
½ tsp ground cinnamon
150 g (5 oz) raisins
1 apple, peeled, cored and diced

Pre-heat an oven to 180°C/350°F/Gas Mark 4. Beat the egg in a bowl and mix together with the sunflower oil and milk. In a large mixing bowl, mix together all the remaining ingredients. Pour over the egg mixture and mix until just moistened, taking care not to over mix. Pour into ten muffin cups lined with paper cases and bake in the oven for 25 minutes.

Summer fruit yoghurt ice cream

This creamy frozen yoghurt tastes wonderful and it's made with good healthy ingredients.
You could also make it using fresh summer fruits.

**300 g (10 oz) mixed frozen summer fruits, e.g. raspberries, blackberries, blueberries,
strawberries, cherries, redcurrants**
400 ml (14 fl oz) mild natural yoghurt
200 ml (7 fl oz) double (thickened) cream
75 g (3 oz) caster sugar plus 1 tbsp

Purée and sieve half the summer fruits. Stir the yoghurt if it is set yoghurt and lightly whisk
the cream until it forms soft peaks. Mix together the yoghurt, cream, 75 g (3 oz) of the caster
sugar and the summer fruit purée. Freeze in an ice cream-making machine. When frozen, mix
the remaining summer fruits with the remaining tablespoon of caster sugar and stir into the
ice cream mixture.

   Alternatively, spoon into a suitable container and put in the freezer. When half frozen,
beat well until smooth, either with a hand-held electric whisk or in a food processor, to break
down the ice crystals that form. Mix the rest of the fruit with the tablespoon of caster sugar
and stir into the yoghurt ice cream. Return to the freezer and stir one or two more times
during the freezing process to get a smooth ice cream.

*Yoghurt can be used in
place of milk if you are milk
intolerant because the live
bacteria used in the process
of making yoghurt has pre-
digested a lot of the lactose
(milk sugar) that causes
problems in many people.*

SUPERFOODS

Summer fruit milkshake

**350 g (12 oz) defrosted mixed frozen summer fruits, e.g. strawberries, blueberries,
blackberries, morello cherries and redcurrants (or use fresh berries)**
50 g (2 oz) sieved icing sugar
100 ml (3 fl oz) single cream
200 ml (7 fl oz) full-fat milk
ice cubes

Purée and sieve the summer fruits and mix with the icing sugar. Stir in the single cream and
milk. Serve in glasses over some ice cubes.

Milk *is great for children as
it is rich in calcium. Children
will often take milk as a
drink when it is mixed with
other foods, particularly fruit.*

SUPERFOODS

Food allergies

Surveys show that as many as two in ten people believe they react badly to certain foods. However, a detailed government study suggests that only about two in every one hundred people do have unpleasant reactions to food that can be measured. Many people blame food additives, but reactions to food additives are probably at least one hundred times less common than reactions to natural foods such as milk or wheat.

Food allergy generally begins in childhood and can trigger a wide range of symptoms from vomiting, persistent diarrhoea and abdominal pain to eczema, skin rashes and wheezing. With so many symptoms that could have other causes it is often hard to be sure that food is to blame or to find out which food. Reactions may occur immediately after eating a specific food or may be delayed for hours or even days. If you are worried that your child might be allergic to a certain food, you should seek expert medical advice.

An allergic reaction generally occurs when the immune system wrongly perceives a harmless substance as a threat (see above right) and an immune response is triggered, producing a large amount of antibodies in the blood. This can cause or contribute to various conditions such as eczema, urticaria, hay fever, asthma, diarrhoea and even failure to thrive. With the later introduction of solid foods between four and six months, the incidence of food allergy in young babies has become less common. However, it is still babies under the age of eighteen months who are most likely to develop an allergy.

> **Healthy eating:** Milk-free vegetable or soya margarine may be substituted for butter; there are also many soya-based (non-dairy) yoghurts and desserts available, and carob can be substituted for milk chocolate.

The commonest foods that carry a risk of allergic reaction in babies

- **Cow's milk and dairy products.**
- **Nuts.**
- **Eggs.**
- **Wheat-based products.**
- **Fish and shellfish.**
- **Citrus and berry fruits.**

A family history of allergies

There is a lot of anxiety about food allergies. However, unless there is a family history of allergy, food allergies are quite rare. The risk of a child developing an allergic disorder more than doubles if there is a family history of a parent or sibling with an atopic disease such as asthma, eczema or hay fever. In this case, breastfeeding for at least four, and preferably six, months seems to offer some protection. Bear in mind if you are breastfeeding that by eating certain foods like dairy products, eggs, oranges or wheat, the allergic substances may be transmitted through your breast milk. This can then cause a reaction in your baby (like eczema). Don't cut major food groups such as dairy products in your own diet as you may become deficient yourself. Always check with a dietician first.

Do not introduce any foods that might cause an allergy before six months at the earliest. Instead, only start weaning with low-allergen foods like baby rice, root vegetables, apple and pear. Avoid high-risk foods (see list above) until your baby is 9 to 12 months old. If there is a family history of allergy to a particular food, avoid that food until your child is at least one year old. Do not remove key foods from your child's diet without first consulting a doctor. If you suspect that your child is allergic to a common food such as milk or wheat, seek expert advice on planning a balanced diet.

Many children outgrow food allergies by three to five years. However, there is no cure for some life-long allergies and the only way to remain healthy is to avoid the problem food. A young baby's immune system is not fully matured and babies can become ill very quickly, so never hesitate to call a doctor if you are worried.

How to diagnose a food allergy

The only accurate way to diagnose food allergies is to eliminate the suspected or most common allergens, wait for symptoms to cease and after a period of about six weeks, reintroduce them one by one until the symptoms reappear. This is called an elimination diet followed by food challenging. This type of diet should only be done under medical supervision and with the help of a state-registered dietician. Other methods such as electrode testing and skin prick tests are not accurate means of diagnosing food allergies.

Specific food allergies

Cow's milk protein allergy: This is the most commonly occurring allergy in children. An allergic reaction to infant formula or any dairy product can occur in a matter of minutes, or even after a few days to weeks. Symptoms can include cramps, diarrhoea, vomiting, a skin rash or breathing difficulties.

If your baby is sensitive to cow's milk-based infant formula, consult your doctor, who might recommend either a soya-based formula or a specially designed hypoallergenic formula. About 30 per cent of babies who are allergic to cow's milk also become allergic to soya milk. Breast milk is the best milk for babies but breastfeeding mothers will need to eliminate dairy foods from their own diets.

If your child is allergic to cow's milk make sure that any foods you buy do not contain: milk, butter, cheese, cream, yoghurt, ghee, whey, lactose and milk solids.

Food additives and colourings: Some widely used food additives like the food colourings tartrazine have been associated with allergic reactions in a small minority of children. There have also been reported links between hyperactivity and diet. There is some evidence that in a small minority (a much lower incidence than is perceived by parents), additives such as flavourings and colouring or foods such as milk or wheat may change behaviour.

Food intolerance: A food intolerance, sometimes called a false food allergy, is a condition where the body is temporarily incapable of digesting certain foods. It is generally short-lived and is not the same as a true food allergy, which involves the immune system. However, it can provoke the same symptoms, so if you suspect that your child is allergic to a common food like cow's milk, you should consult your paediatrician before changing milk formula. It is quite possible that your baby's reaction is only temporary. If your child is found to be allergic to a basic food like wheat, you should always seek expert advice as to how you can keep meals balanced.

Gluten intolerance: Gluten is found in wheat, rye, barley and oats and is therefore present in foods like bread, pasta and biscuits. Some people suffer from a permanent sensitivity to gluten – a condition known as coeliac disease – which although rare, is a serious medical condition. It is diagnosed medically by a blood test and confirmed by actually looking at the gut wall using endoscopy.

Symptoms of gluten disease include loss of appetite, poor growth, swollen abdomen, pale, bulky, frothy and smelly stools. Foods containing gluten should not be introduced into any baby's diet before six months. Cereals used between four to six months should be gluten free, such as rice or maize. When buying baby cereals and rusks, choose varieties that are gluten free. Baby rice is the safest to try at first, and thereafter there are plenty of alternative gluten-free products such as soya, corn, rice, millet, rice noodles, buckwheat spaghetti and potato flours for thickening and baking.

Peanuts: Peanuts and peanut products can induce a severe allergic reaction called anaphylactic shock, which can be life threatening. In families with a history of any allergy, including hay fever, eczema and asthma, it is advisable to avoid all products containing peanuts until the child is three years old and then seek medical advice before introducing peanut products into the diet. Vegetable oils, which may contain peanut oil, will not cause a reaction as the oil is refined, removing any traces of peanut protein. Provided there is no family history of allergy, peanut butter and finely ground nuts can be introduced from six months. Whole nuts should not be given to children under the age of five because of the risk of choking.

Foods for common ailments

Asthma
See Atopic illnesses.

Atopic illnesses
Breastfeeding will help delay the onset of any of the atopic-type illnesses such as asthma, eczema, food allergies and hay fever. In some cases, dietary changes may alleviate the symptoms but the only way to be certain is to follow an elimination diet.

Colic
Colic is common in babies between six weeks and three months and often is worse in the evenings. The causes of colic are still uncertain but to help alleviate symptoms, some breastfeeding mothers eliminate certain foods from their diets. If individual foods such as raspberries are eliminated this is fine but if major food groups such as dairy products are eliminated, dietetic advice should be sought immediately. Eliminating dairy products, a major source of calcium during breastfeeding, puts a mother at risk of developing serious problems such as osteoporosis or weak bones when she is older.

Coping with colic
• Change the feeding position of your baby to a more upright position and gentle movement may help to settle some babies.
• Alcohol-free gripe water preparations may be given over one month of age.
• Colic drops may be useful.
• Herbal drinks may be given in small amounts as long as they are sugar free (remember dextrose means sugar).
• Massage can help to relieve pain and tension.

Colds and flu
Make sure your child has plenty of fresh fruit and vegetables to ensure a good intake of vitamins and minerals. Look especially to those rich in vitamin C (see page 16). Recent research shows that chicken soup can help reduce mucus, boost immunity and reduce inflammation in the nose – it is easy to swallow and rich in vitamins and minerals.

Constipation
Constipation is the infrequent passing of hard stools every four to eight days. It is very rare in breastfed infants as breast milk is more easily digested and has a laxative effect. Formula-fed infants tend to pass stools less frequently and the stools can be a different colour and consistency. Babies' bowel habits vary, but if you think your baby is constipated, first try ensuring feeds are made up properly and not over-concentrated and offer bottles of cooled, boiled water between milk feeds. Do not add sugar to the feeding bottle as this could make things worse.

Once your baby is weaned, give foods that are naturally rich in fibre, e.g. fruit and vegetables, prunes (fruit and juice), baked beans and lentils. After she is six months old, also give less of the refined foods like white bread and sugary breakfast cereals and give wholemeal bread and wholegrain cereals like Weetabix, porridge and muesli instead. Offer chopped nuts and dried fruit and use wholemeal pasta and brown rice. Avoid stodgy food like rice pudding or macaroni cheese. If the problem persists and is severe, see your GP.

Diarrhoea
Most children suffer with diarrhoea at some point; it is a sign that the body needs to evacuate something that is causing irritation and it may be accompanied by vomiting. There are many possible reasons for diarrhoea. It may be caused by too much fibre or fruit juice in the diet, it may indicate a food sensitivity, or some kind of food poisoning. Diarrhoea can also be a side effect of drugs, particularly antibiotics.

Most children will lose their appetites to some degree when they are unwell. Young children can become seriously dehydrated very quickly, so the important thing is to make sure your child is maintaining his fluid intake. Continue to offer milk feeds and cooled, boiled, water. Very dilute fruit juice can also be used. For babies over six weeks add 1 teaspoon unsweetened fruit juice or baby fruit juice to 60 ml (2 fl oz) cooled, boiled water; for babies over three months add 2 to 3 teaspoons unsweetened fruit juice to 60 ml (2 fl oz) cooled, boiled water.

If the diarrhoea persists then you can try some oral rehydration fluid from your chemist to prevent dehydration. If your baby or child is vomiting as well and unable to keep anything down then contact your GP for further advice.

Sometimes when a child has had diarrhoea for an extended period, he may develop a secondary lactose intolerance. This means that he may become intolerant to the sugar in the milk. This is usually a temporary condition and will resolve by itself once the diarrhoea is improved. Do not stop milk feeds for infants without consulting a health professional first. Babies with diarrhoea still need fluid and nutrition, and milk provides both.

Good foods to give to your child once the diarrhoea has stopped include rice, semolina, grilled fish, banana and toast, plain biscuits and apple purée (see recipe on page 40).

Eczema

Eczema is a complicated subject and children with eczema should always be checked out by their GP. There is also an eczema society, which provides information and advice for sufferers and their families. Eczema is often not due to food but other things such as clothes detergents, soaps, grasses or pollens in the air. If a child has an allergic family then breatfeeding may help delay the onset of eczema. The foods most commonly implicated in food allergies that may present as eczema are cow's milk, nuts, wheat, eggs and shellfish (see also pages 182 to 183).

Fever

When your child is unwell and off her food, always give plenty of fluids. Try offering nourishing fluids like milky drinks such as hot chocolate or milkshakes. Clear soups, especially chicken soup, are also good.

Offer your child her favourite foods to stimulate her appetite,

but don't get too worried. Minimal food for a few days will not have a serious impact on your child's health and most children will make up for it by eating more than usual when they are better.

If your child is on antibiotics, offer live yoghurt. Antibiotics kill off both bad and good bacteria in the intestine and eating live yoghurt helps restore the good bacteria.

Food allergies

See Atopic illnesses and pages 182 to 183.

Hay fever

See Atopic illnesses.

Lactose intolerance

Lactose intolerance is sometimes – incorrectly – thought to be an allergy. In fact, lactose is the sugar in milk and lactose intolerance is the inability to digest this sugar because of a lack of a digestive enzyme called lactase in the gut. The main symptoms are diarrhoea, cramping, flatulence and abdominal distension. Lactose intolerance can be hereditary, where the body simply does not produce sufficient amount of lactase, or lactose intolerance can follow a period of gastroenteritis (infection in the gut). Following gastroenteritis, the sites where the enzyme lactase is produced may be damaged and therefore the lactose remains undigested, causing problems. In a few weeks to months, the enzyme begins to be produced again and lactose is digested normally again.

Children with lactose intolerance should avoid dairy products and either consume at least 600 ml (20 fl oz) of calcium-fortified soya milk daily plus calcium-rich foods or take a calcium supplement, which can be prescribed by their doctor. Recently low-lactose formulas and low-lactose milks have been designed for lactose intolerance.

Wind

See Colic.

Index

Annabel Karmel is the author of fourteen best-selling books on nutrition and cooking for babies, children and families. A mother of three, she has been hugely influential in her imaginative approach to creating healthy food that also tastes good.

Her first book, *The Complete Baby and Toddler Meal Planner*, written in 1991, has become the definitive, authoritative guide on feeding babies and children and is now sold worldwide. Endorsed by Great Ormond Street Hospital, the UK's leading children's hospital, total sales are now in excess of several million and the book remains steadily in the top 5 list of best-selling cookery books in the UK.

Since writing her first book, she has written many other best-selling books covering nutrition and recipes for all ages, from *Top 100 Baby Purées* and *Lunchboxes* to the *After School Meal Planner* and *Favourite Family Recipes*. She has also written a comprehensive parenting guide, *The Complete First Year Planner*, covering all the practicalities from eating in pregnancy to getting your baby to sleep through the night.

Annabel is the expert in getting your child, no matter how fussy, to eat a healthier diet – without even noticing! She has developed ways to get children to improve their diet – from hiding vegetables in other foods, packing powerhouse lunchboxes and creating healthy junk food – without the need for parents to spend hours in the kitchen.

Annabel has recently launched 'Eat Fussy', a range of delicious, nutritious, fresh ready-meals for 1- to 4-year-olds, made from 100 per cent natural ingredients. She has also developed a range of equipment and food for Boots, 'Make Your Own', designed to help mums prepare their own fresh baby food by combining freshness with convenience.

Annabel writes regularly for a broad spectrum of national publications including *The Times*, *Mail* and *Sunday Mirror*, *Practical Parenting*, *BBC Good Food* and *Sainsbury's Magazine*. She is the children's celebrity chef on the BBC website and also appears frequently on radio and television as an expert on nutritional issues, including BBC Breakfast News, Sky News, BBC1's *Saturday Kitchen*, and the 'Foodie Godmother' series for Richard and Judy. Annabel was one of eight Iconic British Chefs selected for a series for *This Morning*.

Annabel was awarded an MBE in June 2006 in the Queen's Birthday Honours List for her outstanding work in the field of child nutrition.

Visit Annabel's website at www.annabelkarmel.com

Author's acknowledgements

To my three children, Nicholas, Lara and Scarlett, who have chomped through the pages of this book with gusto.

To my husband Simon, whose expertise in the eating of baby food is unsurpassed.

To my mother Evelyn Etkind, who frequently raids my fridge for the benefit of her dinner parties.

To David Karmel for his late-night rescue missions to retrieve my day's output from the recycle bin.

To Daniel Pangbourne for his fabulous photography. He brings food to life and manages to keep children still.

To Jacqui Barnett for her tireless support and enthusiasm.

To Paul Sacher from Great Ormond Street Children's Hospital.

To Marina Magpoc, Letty Catada and Jane Hamilton, a special big thank you for all your help.

Gail Rebuck, Amelia Thorpe, Denise Bates, Lisa Pendreigh, Emma Callery, Helen Lewis, Sarah Lewis, Tessa Evelegh, Jo Pratt, Borra Garson, Stephen Springate.

To my wonderful models Amelia Arkhurst, Louis Fattal, Somerset Francis, Jo Glick, Scarlett Karmel, Lucas Keusey, Olivia Leigh, Anouska Levy, Alexandra Meller, Harry Ross and Arabella Schild.

The publishers would also like to thank the following for the loan of props in this book: Heal's, 196 Tottenham Court Road, London W1P 9LD and branches (nursery furniture); Muji, 6 Tottenham Court Road, London W1 and branches (baby clothes), Babygap, branches countrywide (baby clothes) and Bridgewater, 739 Fulham Road, London SW6 5UL (pottery).

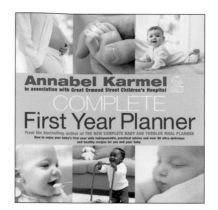

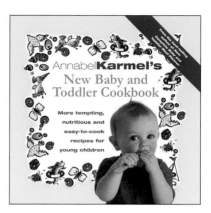

Annabel Karmel:
the number 1, best-selling author on cooking for children

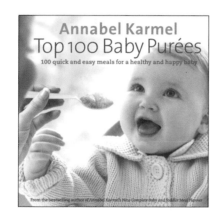

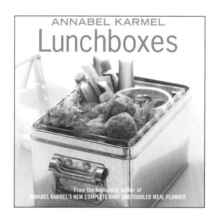

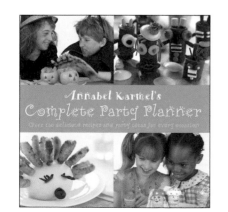

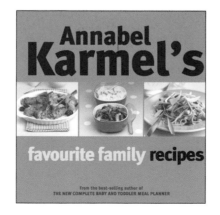

Annabel Karmel's
make your own ...

I recognise that how you feed your baby is one of the most important decisions you make for your child, so I have devised a new range of equipment and food to help you. The range provides everything you need to make fresh food for your baby or toddler. It includes:

- Baby Food Grinder
- Electric Hand Blender
- Food Cube Trays
- Rocket Ice Lolly Moulds
- Sauces and Pastas

All are available from Boots stores and from www.Boots.com. For delicious recipes from the range, visit my website www.annabelkarmel.com

It's good to be a bit fussy about what you eat these days. That's why I have created a new range of tasty, yet healthy meals made especially for children. They're balanced, mouth-watering meals for young children without the fuss. What's more, I'm very fussy about what goes into them so I only use the best natural ingredients.

- Scrummy Chicken Dumplings with Rice
- Mummy's Favorite Salmon and Cod Fish Pie
- Beef Cottage Pie
- Yummy Chicken Curry
- Hidden Vegetable Pasta
- Cheeky Chicken and Potato Pie
- Teddy Bear Pizzas

Look for Eat Fussy in the chilled section of your local supermarket: just ask!